Ali Baba and the Forty Thieves

A Basic Pantomime

Trudy West

A SAMUEL FRENCH ACTING EDITION

FOUNDED 1830

SAMUELFRENCH-LONDON.CO.UK
SAMUELFRENCH.COM

Copyright © 1948 by Trudy West
All Rights Reserved

ALI BABA AND THE FORTY THIEVES is fully protected under the copyright laws of the British Commonwealth, including Canada, the United States of America, and all other countries of the Copyright Union. All rights, including professional and amateur stage productions, recitation, lecturing, public reading, motion picture, radio broadcasting, television and the rights of translation into foreign languages are strictly reserved.

ISBN 978-0-573-06406-7

www.samuelfrench-london.co.uk

www.samuelfrench.com

FOR AMATEUR PRODUCTION ENQUIRIES

UNITED KINGDOM AND WORLD EXCLUDING NORTH AMERICA

plays@SamuelFrench-London.co.uk

020 7255 4302/01

Each title is subject to availability from Samuel French,

depending upon country of performance.

CAUTION: Professional and amateur producers are hereby warned that *ALI BABA AND THE FORTY THIEVES* is subject to a licensing fee. Publication of this play does not imply availability for performance. Both amateurs and professionals considering a production are strongly advised to apply to the appropriate agent before starting rehearsals, advertising, or booking a theatre. A licensing fee must be paid whether the title is presented for charity or gain and whether or not admission is charged.

The professional rights in this play are controlled by Samuel French Ltd, 52 Fitzroy Street, London, W1T 5JR.

No one shall make any changes in this title for the purpose of production. No part of this book may be reproduced, stored in a retrieval system, or transmitted in any form, by any means, now known or yet to be invented, including mechanical, electronic, photocopying, recording, videotaping, or otherwise, without the prior written permission of the publisher. No one shall upload this title, or part of this title, to any social media websites.

The right of Trudy West to be identified as author of this work has been asserted by him in accordance with Section 77 of the Copyright, Designs and Patents Act 1988

PREFACE.

Of all our national forms of entertainment, the Pantomime is perhaps the most traditional and shows least signs of waning popularity. The average " run " of the professional pantomime is certainly as long as ever, and for many years it has been a source of considerable enjoyment and profit among amateur societies.

It is for this latter field of activity that this series of " BASIC PANTOMIME " has been specially designed, both as regards the " scripts," the settings, and the general production problems which face every company in work of this type.

Apart from the time-honoured stories on which all our pantomimes are (and rightly) based, much of their success depends on topicality, local and current humour, and by no means least upon the songs and choruses of the time—even of the year.

With this in view, these " basic " pantomimes have been prepared, not as the final, unalterable show, but as *bases* upon which may be built the ultimate product according to the desires, and the resources, of the individual company.

The scripts follow, in each case, the traditional stories very strictly. Any major departure would be resented by the youngest—and the oldest ! —members of the audience. The dialogue is in modern prose, and prepared so that " cuts," additions, and the introduction of " local " or " topical " references may be effected with a minimum of difficulty.

Simplicity has been the prior aim also with regard to the settings, which are dealt with in detail in the " Production Notes " for each of the scripts. These contain suggestions for yet further simplification where the exigencies of the theatre are exceptionally limited, as well as indications of elaboration for those who are more fortunately placed.

Equal consideration has been given to the matter of Musical Numbers, Dances, etc. Those indicated represent what may be regarded as a reasonable minimum; in fact, where resources are available, one or two extra numbers might be added with advantage. But the basic form which the pantomimes take render these additions quite easy to effect.

On the other hand, it will be found that, if desired, the pantomimes may be produced without alteration in any department despite the title of " BASIC " which has, for the foregoing reasons, been conferred upon them.

CHARACTERS:

ALI BABA (a poor camel driver).

SELIMA (his wife).

KEMAL HAROUN (his son).

MORGIANA (his servant maid).

CASSIM BABA (Ali's rich brother).

NELLA (Cassim's wife).

HEELAM (a cobbler).

MUSTAPHA DUBBUHL (a fishmonger).

MUSTAPHA NUTHA (a greengrocer).

AL RASCHOUN (the Robber Chief of the Forty Thieves).

SMASHEM
GRABBEM } (two of the Forty Thieves).

A FLOWER SELLER.

ROSETTI
GOGETTI } (Slave Girls of Cassim Baba).

A PEDLAR.

Various Tradesmen, Townspeople, The Forty Thieves, a Snake Charmer, Dancers, Water Carriers, and others.

SYNOPSIS OF SCENES.

ACT I.

SCENE 1. *The Street of the Bazaars.*
SCENE 2. *A Cave in the Desert.*
SCENE 3. *As in Scene 1.*

ACT II.

SCENE 1. *The Cave in the Desert.*
SCENE 2. *The Street of the Bazaars.*
SCENE 3. *The Same.*

ACT III.

SCENE 1. *A Room in Ali Baba's New House.*
SCENE 2. *The Stable of Ali's House.*
SCENE 3. *As in Scene 1.*

MUSICAL NUMBERS.

Opportunities for about twenty-one Musical Numbers have been provided in the book.

For six of these lyrics have been provided, set to well-known airs, as follows :—

No. 1. Opening Chorus. (*Air :* " *What Shall We Do With the Drunken Sailor?*")

No. 6. Robbers' Chorus. (*Air :* "*Amo, Amas, I love a Lass.*") ("*Songs of England*" *Vol.* 2. *Boosey*).

No. 8. "Open, Sesame!" (*Air :* " *The Poacher* ").

No. 10. " Secrets " (*Air :* " *Tobacco is an Indian Weed.*")

No. 11. " Brains." (*Air :* " *Here's to the Maiden of Bashful Fifteen.*")

No. 14. "Ali Baba's Rich To-day." (*Air :* " *Boys and Girls Come Out to Play.*")

For the rest, popular songs and choruses can be found without difficulty.

As in all " Basic " pantomimes, the Numbers may be reduced or added to at will.

Incidental and dance music, however, should have a very pronounced Eastern character.

Act I.

1. Opening Chorus .. (Full Company)
2. Comedy Quartette .. (Dubbuhl, Nutha, Rosetti, Gogetti)
3. Duet .. .. .. (Ali Baba *and* Selima)

4. Song .. .. .. (Morgiana)
5. Duet .. .. .. (Kemal *and* Morgiana)
6. The Robbers' Chorus (Al Raschoun *and* Robbers)
7. Scena : Chant, Chorus and Dance (Snake Charmer *and* Chorus)
8. Song : "Open, Sesame!" (Ali Baba *and* Principals)

Act II.

9. Dance of the Desert Spirits (*The* Spirits)
10. Song : " Secrets " .. (Heelam *and* Chorus)
11. Comedy Duet "Brains" (Smashem *and* Grabbem)
12. Duet .. .. .. (Kemal *and* Morgiana)
13. Ensemble .. .. (The Revellers)
14. Ensemble : "Ali Baba's Rich To-day " .. (Ali *and* Chorus)

Act III.

15. Duet .. .. .. (Ali Baba *and* Selima)
16. Concerted Number .. (Principals *and* Chorus)
17. Song .. .. .. (Kemal)
18. Song .. .. .. (Morgiana)
19. Chorus .. .. (Full Company)
20. The Dagger Dance.. (Morgiana)
21. Grand Finale .. (The Full Company)

PRODUCTION NOTES.

The "Basic" version of ALI BABA requires only two full sets, and two "half" sets, and the furnishing of these is exceptionally simple.

The pantomime presents considerable opportunity for Oriental effects, which may be as picturesque and "extravagant" as you please. In fact, it is almost impossible to overdo the Orientalism.

There is only one "magical" effect, namely, the rising snake for the Snake Charmer. An invisible wire may be attached to the snake in the box, and be drawn up slowly. Alternatively, any conjurer's store will supply a simple apparatus.

The first setting to be considered is :—

THE STREET OF THE BAZAARS.

This is used for :—Act 1. Scene 1.
Act 1. Scene 3.
Act 2. Scene 2.
Act 2. Scene 3.

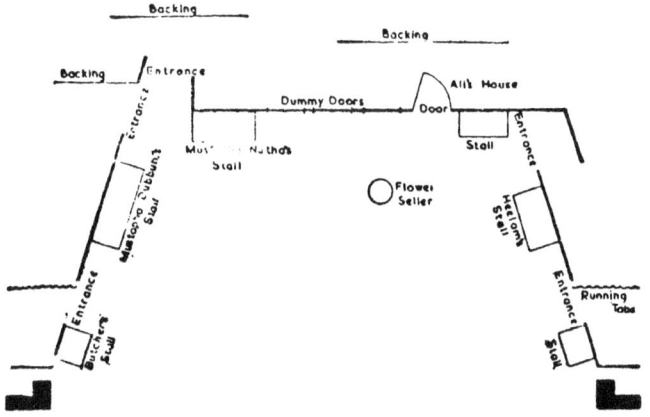

It consists of a wall across the back, which should be plain " off-white " or pale stone colour. There should be two or three " dummy " doors, but the last one (up L.C.) is practical, and leads into Ali Baba's house.

There is an exit up R., giving the impression of a street going upstage, with a turning off R. also. Another exit up L., above HEELAM's stall. Exits downstage R. and L.

The stalls are set as in the ground plan and should be well stocked with goods according to the specified trades. Each stall should have a gaily coloured awning which can be lowered for the scenes which are not in shopping hours.

Next, we have the " Cave Scene." This may be a half set and the Bazaar setting need not be much disturbed in order to set it.

This is for Act I, Scene 1, and Act II, Scene 1.

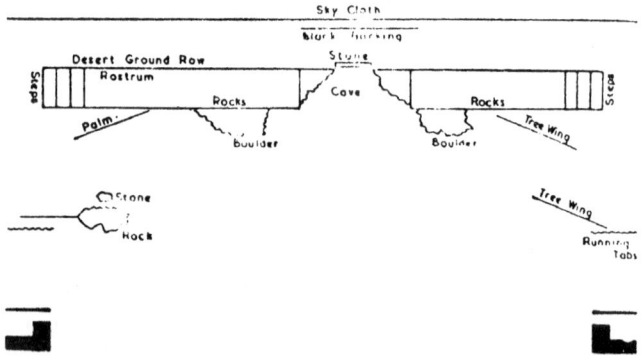

It consists of a plain sky-cloth, below which is a rocky ground row, rising more steeply at C., where the mouth of the cave is set.

Above the ground row, on each side of the " cave " should be a rostrum on which the SPIRITS appear in silhouette against the sky.

The Cave must have a sliding door, opened by stage hands from behind, and representing a stone. This must be backed with black, and unlit from within.

Two boulders are needed, and a rock which is just high enough to conceal ALI when the Robbers are on stage.

Palm and tree wings complete the setting.

We now come to :—

A ROOM IN ALI BABA'S NEW HOUSE.

This is used in Act III only—Scenes 1 and 3, and will be set between Acts II and III, and thereafter left undisturbed.

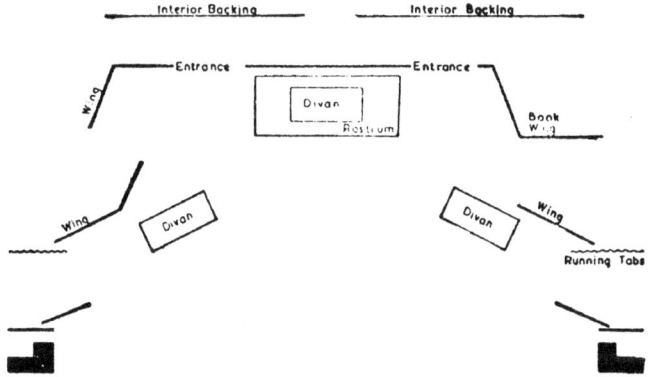

If desired, a curtain setting may be used—indeed, this may be both more effective and easier to provide.

A rostrum up C. is desirable if it can be managed. Three backless " oriental " divans are needed, and should be provided with gorgeously coloured draperies and cushions.

The simple properties needed are in the Property Plot.

Lastly, we have :—

THE STABLE OF ALI BABA'S HOUSE.

This is for Act III, Scene 2. It is a half set.

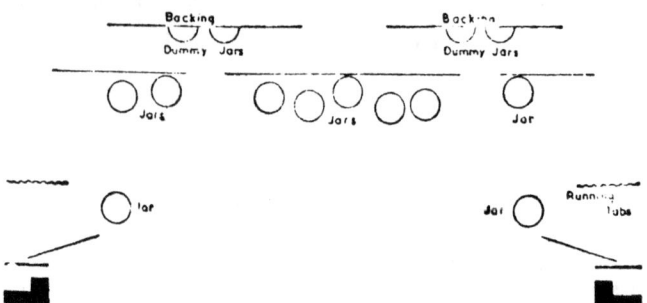

A cut-cloth will serve, painted to represent a stone wall, or the interior of a stable. The " cuts " are well to R. and L. Two plain wings, or " legs " down R. and down L., are all that is needed to complete it.

The " jars " could be hired. Alternatively, they are not difficult to construct. They need not be complete jars, but merely dummy fronts. Should they not be substantial enough to climb into from the top, they may have hinged doors (front or side) and the Robbers enter thereby.

The backings behind the " cuts " should, if possible, suggest the existence of many other jars behind the wall, into which the Robbers are presumed to go. In this connection we would remind the producer that the slaves should run in and out of the cuts, apparently to fill the many jars presumed to be set there.

The lighting of the pantomime may be as elaborate as the producer can devise. A simple lighting plot, as a basic guide, is provided.

ACT I*

SCENE 1.

SCENE.—*The Street of the Bazaars.*

(*See the Ground Plan*)

When the CURTAIN *rises, the stage is full of traders—some at the stalls, others itinerant, moving among the crowd —customers, slaves, etc. They are chanting the air of the opening number, and there is much movement, action, chatter, and laughter.*

No. 1. OPENING NUMBER .. (FULL COMPANY)
(AIR : " *What Shall We Do With the Drunken Sailor ?*")

TRADERS. Come along folk, the day is dawning
Plenty of goods on sale this morning
You ain't got long—we give you warning
It's our Early Closing !

(*Nasally, with Oriental bus.*)

Haiya ! Come and buy-ah !
Haiya ! Come and buy-ah !
Haiya ! Come and buy-ah !
'Cos it's Early Closing !

CUSTOMERS. What have you got for sale, my masters ?
What have you got for two piastres ?

DUBBHI. ⎫ (*together*). ⎧ Pickled eels' feet and mustard
NUTHA ⎭ ⎩ plasters !

ALL. 'Cos it's Early Closing !
Haiya ! Come and buy-ah ! (*Etc., etc.*)

TRADERS. Petticoats, sago, sandals, spices,
Cauliflower, bed-spreads, socks and ices,
Second-hand cheese at bargain prices
'Cos it's Early Closing !
Haiya ! Come and buy-ah ! (*Etc., etc.*)

---

*N.B. Paragraph 3 on page ii of this Acting Edition regarding photocopying and video-recording should be carefully read.

(DANCE. *Exeunt after Dance all except the Principals playing in the ensuing scene.* When the CROWD *has gone, only* MUSTAPHA DUBBUHL, MUSTAPHA NUTHA, HEELAM, *a* BUTCHER, *a* FLOWER-SELLER, *and a* PEDLAR *are left on the stage.*)

M. DUBBUHL. Well, O Mustapha Nutha, that's all for the day. Early closing! What a beautiful thought!

M. NUTHA. Indeed, O Mustapha Dubbuhl! It soothes the mind like the scent of lotus flowers beneath the shadow of a date palm!

M. DUBBUHL. You're telling me! Are they open yet at "The Caliph's Arms"?

M. NUTHA. Soon — soon, O Thou of Unquenchable Thirstiness! It is nigh on noon!

M. DUBBUHL. Wait for it—wait for it! See what's coming!

(*Enter*, L., ROSETTI *and* GOGETTI, *two beautiful young slave-girls. Instantly the merchants spring to life and start crying their wares ad. lib.*)

BUTCHER (*dismally*). Cat's meat! Cat's meat! Fresh cat's meat!

ROSETTI (*as she passes*). Away! My mistress has no cats!

BUTCHER. No cats?

GOGETTI. No—they have the evil eye! Away!

DUBBUHL } (*together*). } Away!
NUTHA

(*They eye the girls, glance at each other, and rub their hands.*)

BUTCHER. What—me?
ALL. Yes!
BUTCHER. Oh. Very well.

(*He exits* L.)

FLOWER-SELLER. Flowers, O beauteous ladies?
GOGETTI *and* ROSETTI (*together*). Away!
FLOWER-SELLER. Me, too?

(DUBBUHL and NUTHA, *business anticipating being left alone with the girls.*)

ALL. Away!
FLOWER-SELLER. Sorreh, ayme shaw!

(*She exits* L.)

NUTHA. Dubbuhl, we're all right.
DUBBUHL. I think so! I think so!
HEELAM. Soles to mend! Sandal straps! AND DON'T YOU SAY "AWAY" TO ME! I'm going to sleep—in a minute. (*He bawls.*) *Knives to grind!*
ROSETTI. Knives to grind? You're a cobbler.
HEELAM. Well, anything for a change. Yesterday I cried "Tips for the Camel Races at Gat-week-ah." Queue in no time. Don't wake me. (*He beckons the girls, who draw nearer.*) Be careful of those two. It'll be no use your screaming.
PEDLAR (*suddenly, to nobody in particular, shouting*). AWAY!

(*Everybody staggers and looks at him.*)

Meaning me. Good afternoon. (*He goes* R.)
GOGETTI. But I want some elastic!
PEDLAR. Elastic? Never 'eard of it.

(*He exits* R.)

NUTHA. That'll larn her!
DUBBUHL. She'll manage somehow. (*To the* GIRLS.) Are you not, O Fair-Ones-like-unto-the-lotus-flowers in-(*local park*), the slaves of Lady Nella, wife of Cassim Baba, may the vultures pluck his bones?
ROSETTI. Slaves? I beg yours! We are her lady helps!
DUBBUHL (*business*). Sorreh Ay spoke!
NUTHA (*business*). No offence, Ayme shaw!
GOGETTI. The Lady Nella will be here shortly, requiring fish. But as she wants it fresh, you may as well shut up shop.

(DUBBUHL *reacts.*)

ROSETTI (*to* NUTHA). She wants some dates, but it wouldn't interest you.

(NUTHA *reacts.*)

DUBBUHL (*bringing out property fish*). There's a lovely bit of cod!

(*The* GIRLS *clutch each other, as if fainting.*)

Caught last Tuesday, and it's only Saturday now. With this nice warm weather it's just right for eating.
ROSETTI. Did you say " right "—or " ripe " ?
DUBBUHL (*business*). O Allah! I won't lose my temper—I won't—I *won't*!
NUTHA. Tell me, Fair Gazelles, do you like the firm you're working for?
GOGETTI. No. Cassim Baba is mean, and Lady Nella beats us. But of course, they're very important people.

(MORGIANA, *Ali Baba's slave, enters up* L.C. *from* ALI'S *house.*)

ROSETTI. And the food is excellent. Plenty of dates, garlick, turkish delight, olive oil, bananas, gherkins . . .
DUBBUHL. Chocolates—pea-nuts—programme—book of the words two piastres—Inglis tourist buy curious (*or* " *naughty* ") postcard ? (*Business.*)
GOGETTI (*shouting him down*). And of course we have our evenings off!

(DUBBUHL *and* NUTHA *change their manner.*)

DUBBUHL }
NUTHA   } (*together*). { And which might those evenings be?
ROSETTI }
GOGETTI } (*together*). A-ah!

(DUBBUHL *and* NUTHA *echo this.*)

ROSETTI (*after looking* MORGIANA *up and down over her shoulder*). At least it's better than working for—say—Ali Baba, Cassim's poor brother. I wouldn't work *there*!

MORGIANA. Well, I would! Ali Baba may be poor, but at least they are happy, and content—and *honest*!
ROSETTI. And of course they have a handsome son!
GOGETTI. Kemal Haroun Baba! A camel-driver like his father! (*She laughs.*)
ROSETTI. And is learning wood-carving! Wood carving—I ask you!

(*She laughs, cattily.* DUBBUHL *and* NUTHA *mimic her. Business.*)

GOGETTI. Don't worry, Morgiana, Ali Baba will never let his fine son marry his slave!
MORGIANA. Beasts! (*She hurries into the house.*)
DUBBUHL. What a lady! Well, as your lady Nella hasn't turned up, I'm closing. (*He shuts down the cover of his stall.*)
ROSETTI. Aren't you putting your fish on ice?
DUBBUHL. I'm a business man. I keep my fish in a nice warm stall, and then, when I open up in the morning, everyone knows it's there. (*He holds his nose.*) It pays to advertise!
NUTHA. And now perhaps you girls will join us at " The Caliph's Arms " for a little dinky-winky? (*He puts his arm round* ROSETTI.)
DUBBUHL. Just a ickle dinky-winky? (*He puts his arm round* GOGETTI.)
ROSETTI. Only the very best wine agrees with me.
GOGETTI. Quaite.
DUBBUHL (*to* NUTHA). Wine!
NUTHA. Wine! Not nice beer?
ROSETTI. For girls like us, only the best is good enough!
DUBBUHL. Chum—we've had it!

NO. 2 QUARTETTE .. DUBBUHL, NUTHA, ROSETTI, GOGETTI.

(*After the Number, they* DANCE.)

MUSIC. *Enter* CASSIM BABA *and his wife*, NELLA. *They are richly dressed. Everything about* NELLA *is exaggerated. As they make their majestic entrance,* DUBBUHL, NUTHA, *and the* GIRLS *bow low, foreheads to the ground.*

GIRLS. Salaam, O Protectors of the Poor! Salaam! Salaam!

NUTHA
DUBBUHL } *(together).* { Salaam! O Vision of Loveliness and Lord of Incalculable Wealth and Generosity—*(aside)* we hope!

NELLA. Rise!

NUTHA
DUBBUHL } *(together).* Eh?

NELLA. I said—Rise!

NUTHA
DUBBUHL } *(rising together).* { Okay. O Mistress of Ineffable Condescension!

(NELLA *waves* ROSETTI *and* GOGETTI *away. The two girls exeunt up* R.)

DUBBUHL. O Lady of Infinite Circumspection, thou owest us for two months' fish!

CASSIM. Oh, dear! I think we ought to pay, dear.

NELLA (*to* CASSIM). Don't be absurd! (*To* DUBBUHL.) How much?

DUBBUHL. Forty dinas.

NELLA. Forty dinas! But I have discount!

DUBBUHL. Lady, I have taken off the discount!

NELLA. There is a saying in the East—a good deed done is a good deed. But a good deed done twice is better. So take the discount off again, O Mustapha Dubbuhl!

DUBBUHL. In other words, you must have a double from Mustapha Dubbuhl! Thirty-five dinas.

NELLA. Pay him, Cassim!

CASSIM (*crossing to* DUBBUHL). And my commission as agent?

DUBBUHL (*weakly*). Five dinas.

CASSIM (*paying him*). Thank you.

NUTHA. And don't worry about *my* bill! Not as things are going to-day! Excuse us—we have a pressing engagement! (*He looks up the street.*) At least, I think we have. (*He sees the girls.*) Yes, we have!

DUBBUHL. And we could do with it!

NUTHA and DUBBUHL. Good morning!

(*They straighten their headdresses, smooth down their gowns and similar business; then they march off to music.*)

NELLA. Really, tradesmen become more insolent every day.
CASSIM. Did you say insolent, dear, or insolvent?
NELLA. INSOLENT!
CASSIM. Oh!

(*Enter* ALI BABA *from his house, singing merrily. He stops, on seeing* NELLA *and* CASSIM.)

CASSIM. Ah, brother Ali Baba, do you go to work again today?
ALI BABA. I do, brother Cassim, I do! I take my one poor camel to Mukka-dada to fetch a bale of silk for Golapha Pasha.
NELLA. It's a pity my husband's brother still has to work! And *such* work! It lets the family down so.
ALI BABA. It's honest work, I like it, and am happy. What more could I ask?
NELLA. What more? Well, if you don't know, that finishes it.
CASSIM (*taking* ALI BABA *aside*). You should have married a rich wife, as I did, Ali. Why, I'm the richest man in Baghdad now. (*He rubs his hands greedily.*)
ALI BABA. Ah, but are you the happiest? You needn't answer! My Selima is good enough for me—I wouldn't exchange her for all the wealth of Persia. (*Turning.*) And here she comes, bless her ragged sandals! And I'll be bound she's brought my lunch.

(SELIMA *enters with* MORGIANA, *who carries food packets, water bottles, etc.*)

SELIMA. Good morning, Cassim. Good morning, Nella. Here, Ali, my turtle dove, is your lunch, and that of Kemal, who is to travel with you.
ALI BABA (*to* CASSIM). I am taking Kemal, my son, since it is a very large bale to fetch, and I may have to hire another camel at Mukka-dada.

(MORGIANA *brings the lunch to* ALI, *who takes it; she bows low to him and smiles.*)

Thank you, Morgiana.

NELLA. Come, Cassim, we can't stay all day talking to your poor relations. They'll be wanting to borrow something in a minute.

ALI BABA. No, lady Nella, I do not borrow. But I am always pleased to lend.

NELLA. Lend?

ALI BABA. A little politeness, if you are short of it.

NELLA (*furiously, pushing* MORGIANA *aside*). Out of my way, slave!

(*She goes off.*)

CASSIM. Oh dear, now I shall have this all day and all night too!

NELLA (*off*). Cassim!

CASSIM. Coming, O Rosebud of Inescapable Verbosity! Coming!

(*He goes off.* ALI BABA, SELIMA *and* MORGIANA *laugh heartily.* MORGIANA *bows to them both and goes into the house.*)

SELIMA. I wonder why Cassim and Nella are always so unfriendly? The more riches they get the more unhappy they seem to become—and the ruder.

ALI BABA. It is always so, my turtle dove of Indescribable Grace and Kindness. But I would risk a little unhappiness even with you, if we could but have a little more money, when I think of the lovely things I could buy you! The dresses, the jewels!

SELIMA. I have enough, O Ali of Ridiculous Beneficence, if I have *thy* love!

No. 3. DUET .. .. .. ALI BABA *and* SELIMA.

(*After the Number they exeunt into the house. As they open the door,* MORGIANA *appears.*)

ALI BABA. See if you can find our son, Kemal, O Morgiana, and hasten him. It is time we departed.

MORGIANA. I will, O my master.

(ALI BABA *and* SELIMA *go into the house.*)

MORGIANA (*going to the* L. *exit*). He is not there! (*She runs to the* R. *exit.*) He is not there! Perhaps he is dallying at the Garden of Palms with some fairer maiden than I. And why not? For I am but his father's slave, and of no account whatever. (*She sits on the stone seat* L.C.)

HEELAM (*awakening*). Don't be too sure.

MORGIANA. I beg your pardon, O Cobbler of Amazing Impudence?

HEELAM. I say, don't be too sure. You may be of much account to that young man, Kemal Haroun. I have seen him eye thee with sheep's eyes that speak of love.

MORGIANA. I know. But I am only a slave.

HEELAM. A beggar once became a Caliph through faithful service. Take heed—and serve. A slave may become a lady.

MORGIANA. And a Cobbler a philosopher!

HEELAM. Anything for a change. Good afternoon.

(*He saunters off* L.)

MORGIANA. I wonder! Oh, it would be so lovely!

No. 4. SONG .. .. .. MORGIANA.

(*As the last verse of the song ends,* KEMAL HAROUN, *the son of* ALI BABA, *enters* R. *and listens. He is young, handsome, neatly though poorly dressed. When the song ends, he goes to* MORGIANA *with outstretched arms. She turns and sees him and bows very low.*)

KEMAL. Morgiana!

MORGIANA (*her head on the ground*). O Master Kemal Haroun!

KEMAL. Oh, do get up, Morgiana. You know how I hate you to bow to me. It is for me to bow to you, O Lily of Unspeakable Daintiness and Grace!

MORGIANA (*rising and turning away*). You must not call me that!

KEMAL. And why not, when I love you so?

MORGIANA (*moving towards the house*). I must go and clean the house. And you must make ready to go with your father.

KEMAL (*pleading and trying to stop her*). Why are you afraid of me, beautiful Morgiana? I say I love you! But you have known that for a long time, haven't you?

MORGIANA. Yes. And—and I love you, O Master of Peculiar Insistence! But there can be no such thing as love between a poor slave and her master's son. Ali Baba would—would kill me if he knew!

KEMAL. My father could not kill a chicken! I know he would not consent to our marriage—yet. But once I am a master of wood-carving, and have my own business, then I can do as I like. And something—something surely will happen one day to show that you are somebody better than a slave. My father Ali will see it. My mother Selima will see it! And then! Then . . .!

MORGIANA. Dreams! Dreams! But then—surely it is not wrong to have one's dreams?

No. 5. DUET .. .. .. MORGIANA *and* KEMAL.

(*At the end of the Number,* MORGIANA *is again making a low obeisance to* KEMAL *when* ALI BABA *enters.*)

ALI BABA. Come, Kemal! What! Singing here with a slave girl! This won't do! We take the road to Mukkadada! Come! The camel waits. Morgiana, your mistress also waits. The peace upon you!

MORGIANA (*not rising*). And on you, Masters, the peace! And safe return.

ALI BABA. Come, Kemal.

(ALI BABA *goes off* R. KEMAL, *seeing* ALI BABA *has gone, comes to* MORGIANA. *They embrace.*)

KEMAL. Farewell, Peach Blossom!

MORGIANA. Farewell, Master as Stalwart as a Young Palm Tree!

(*They embrace again.*)

ALI BABA (*off*). Kemal! Hasten—and hasten!

Sc. 1]   ALI BABA   11

KEMAL (*tearing himself from* MORGIANA'S *arms*). I come, father.

He runs off R. MORGIANA *goes into a reprise of the duet refrain as—*

the TABS *close*.

MUSTAPHA DUBBUHL, MUSTAPHA NUTHA, ROSETTI, GO-GETTI, *and other characters enter* R. *and* L. *in front of the* TABS, *dancing. This may be a reprise of No.* 2. *After the Number : Exeunt*.

The TABS *open*.

Scene 2.

Scene.—*A lonely spot in the desert.*

The ground rises to the back, showing a sky line beyond. Slightly L. *of* C. *there is a cave in the side of a rock. The mouth of the cave is covered by a stone slab. Down* R. *is another tall rock behind which is a large stone which, when mounted, enables one to look over the top of the rock.*

When the Curtain *rises,* Ali Baba *enters, followed by* Kemal. *They carry their luncheons and seem weary.*

Ali Baba. Oh, Kemal, I am tired of this kind of life. I'm always trying to make it easier—that is why I took the new road, thinking it was shorter. But it doesn't seem so.

Kemal. Indeed, my father, it seems longer to me.

Ali Baba. You are right. Let's have our lunch.

(*They sit, cross-legged, at* C., *and begin their meal.*)

Kemal. I wish we could do better for ourselves.

Ali Baba. Indeed, so do I—though I always try to be cheerful before your dear mother. She deserves something better than to be the wife of a poor camel-driver.

Kemal. I was thinking that if I get on well with my wood carving and have my own business, you would not have to work so hard.

Ali Baba (*filling a cup*). You are a good son, Kemal Haroun.

(*He passes the cup to* Kemal.)

Kemal. I might even marry, and we could have a larger house, and my wife could help mother . . .

Ali Baba (*busily eating*). What? And get rid of Morgiana?

Kemal. No, father—you see—*she* would be my wife!

Ali Baba. What? A slave? None of the Babas, humble though they are, have ever married slaves!

Kemal. I think Morgiana, if the truth were known, is something better than a slave. And I—I love her so, father.

ALI BABA. I could not hear of it! (*He drinks.*)
KEMAL. But she is so good—and pretty—and devoted to you and mother.
ALI BABA. We will talk of this later. Wait—wait until we are safe home again with the bales of silk for the merchant.
KEMAL. Very well, father. (*He looks off* R.) Look, do you see that? Horsemen! Coming this way! (*He springs up.*)
ALI BABA (*rising*). Oh wallah wallah, shalamallah wali! (*He looks, off* R.). So they are!

(*Distant shouts and horses' hooves off stage.*)

KEMAL. We must get back to the camel!
ALI BABA (*turning to him*). You get back to the camel! Take him to the old road; there is a wadi half a mile farther on! I will hide here, for I am too old and too fat to run! As soon as you see they have gone, return with the camel and we will go on to Mukka-dada. Listen!

(*The* ROBBERS *are heard off stage singing.*)

> Wallah wallah O Imshallah
> Wallah wallah wali-o!
> Soda, bismuth, peppermint and sulphur
> Wallah, wallah-wallah wali-O! (*Shout.*) HI!

(*The sound of horses' hooves.*)

KEMAL. Father! They are the Robbers of Al Raschoun! The famous Forty Thieves—oh, come with me!
ALI BABA. No, my son! Do as I say! Run, now, and take the camel! I will hide behind this rock. Obey me!
KEMAL. Yes, father. Allah protect you!
ALI BABA. And you too, my son. Go!

(KEMAL *exits* L.)

(*The singing recommences, and the sound of horses comes very near.* ALI BABA *hides behind the rock down* R. *The horses' hooves stop. There is the jangling of harness. The* FORTY THIEVES *enter, singing their refrain. They form up.*)

14   ALI BABA   [ACT I

No. 6. ENSEMBLE .. AL RASCHOUN AND THE FORTY THIEVES.

(Air : "Amo, Amas, I love a lass")

RASCHOUN. These robbers under me, Raschoun,
     Are all extremely naughty!
     We live by crimes, and have at times,
     A membership of forty!
ROBBERS. Wallah, wallah, O Imshallah!
     Wallah, wallah, wali-o!
RASCHOUN. Mayhem, felony, cozenage and murder!
ROBBERS. Wallah, wallah-wallah wali-o!
RASCHOUN. They're robbers owned by me, Raschoun,
     And forty is their number!
     They never shirk their evil work
     In normal hours of slumber!
ROBBERS. Wallah, wallah, O Imshallah!
     Wallah, wallah, wali-o!
RASCHOUN. Arson, larceny, forgery and MURDER!
ROBBERS. Wallah, wallah-wallah wali-o!

(At the end of the second refrain, SMASHEM *and* GRABBEM *enter* R. *They share the third verse, thus :)*

SMASHEM. If you're inclined to criticise . . .
GRABBEM. Our moral degradation . . .

   *(*RASCHOUN *flings* GRABBEM *over to* L.*)*

SMASHEM *(not having seen this).*
    Remember we—lightheartedly . . .
RASCHOUN *(advancing on him).*
    Commit assassination!

(He aims a blow at SMASHEM, *who eludes it.)*

ROBBERS *(softly, with dainty burlesque dance steps).*
    Gracefully we cut your throats
    Daintily we plunder!
    All of which we offer you
    Free of charge . . . *(They stop).*
SMASHEM }
GRABBEM } *(together).* No wonder!

ROBBERS (*fortissimo*).
Wallah wallah O Imshallah !
Wallah, wallah, wali-o !
Sin, depravity, knavery and MURDER !
Wallah, wallah-wallah, wali-o !
(*Shouting*) HI !

(*They go about, slapping each other on the back and exchanging the pass-word, " Hi-di-hi."*)

RASCHOUN (*loudly*). Ho-di-ho !

(*They all stop and attend.*)

RASCHOUN. Now, Smashem and Grabbem !

(SMASHEM *and* GRABBEM *come to attention, trembling.*)

SMASHEM }
GRABBEM } (*together*). Er—yes, my lord ?

RASCHOUN. Have you seen to the horses ?

SMASHEM. I've gug-guggiven them their no-no-nosebags, lord.

RASCHOUN. Do you mean nosebags or no nosebags ?

SMASHEM. I mum-mum-mean n-nosebags !

RASCHOUN. Oh. And you, Grabbem ?

GRABBEM. I've tut-tut-tut-tethered them.

RASCHOUN (*sarcastically*). Well, I hope you tut-tether better than you stut-stutter !

(*The* ROBBERS *roar with laughter.*)

If anything happens to that great white steed I borrowed—I say, BORROWED—from the Sultan of Jamjah yesterday, I'll break every bone in your miserable little bodies !

SMASHEM. Oh, thank you so mum-much ! Bub-but there are no robbers about here, lord, except, of course, your forty faithful followers !

GRABBEM. Fertainly fir ! No fieves I affure you ! (*Wailing and turning away.*) Oh, what'f the matter wiff me ?

RASCHOUN (*roaring with laughter*). No thieves ! No thieves ! D'you hear that, my bold fellows ?

(*The* ROBBERS *roar with laughter again.*)

Well, let's see what burdens my little band of Puritans have managed to lift from the shoulders of the undeserving rich! Come on, now! (*He rubs his hands gleefully.*)

(*The* ROBBERS *begin to undo the parcels and boxes, displaying rich silks, jewels, gold and silver, etc. This is done to a general hubbub, and* ALI BABA *peeps over the rock to watch.* SMASHEM *has a rather small parcel. He undoes several wrappings of tissue paper and produces a diamond necklace.*)

GRABBEM. Coo! Who'd'you get that from?

SMASHEM (*putting his fingers to his lips; aside*). Bought 'em at (*local store*) for five piastres, just to keep the old man happy. What did you get?

GRABBEM (*running to* R. *and bringing in a huge tea chest. He lifts the lid and brings out mounds of shavings, etc., and then a packet of tea.*) A quarter of tea!

SMASHEM. Coo—aren't you a *one*?

RASCHOUN. Have you all unpacked?

ROBBERS (*in chorus*). Yes, my lord! Behold, O Al Raschoun!

RASCHOUN. Splendid! Then we'll store them in the secret cave! (*He turns to the rock up* C. *and shouts.*) OPEN, SESAME!

(*The stone rolls away from the cave. The* ROBBERS, *followed by* AL RASCHOUN, *troop into the cave, taking the spoils.* AL RASCHOUN *waits at the mouth of the cave until all are in.*)

SHUT, SESAME!

(AL RASCHOUN *withdraws within the cave and the stone rolls over it once more.* ALI BABA *creeps out from the rock down* R. *wiping his brow.*)

ALI BABA. Have I been dreaming? Where have they gone? I fear to wait and yet am too weak to move! I hope Kemal will not return till they have gone! The Robbers of Al Raschoun! And there, within the cave, their riches—wealth untold!

(*Rumblings within the cave and* AL RASCHOUN'S *voice.* ALI BABA *scuttles back behind the rock* R.)

RASCHOUN (*off*). OPEN, SESAME!

(*The stone rolls away.* AL RASCHOUN *and the* ROBBERS *emerge.*)

And now, away! To Mukka-dada! I hear great bales of rare silks are to be brought today from there to Baghdad!
(*There are shouts of delight. The* ROBBERS *form up.*)
RASCHOUN (*singing*).
 We've stored our stuff, the fruit of bluff
 And violence alarming!
 We may seem rough—our methods tough,
 But life, we find, is charming!
 (*As they march out.*)
 Wallah, wallah, O Imshallah,
 Wallah, wallah, wali-o!
 Mayhem, felony, forgery and MURDER!
 Wallah! Wallah-wallah, wali-o!

(*The* ROBBERS *march out, singing the refrain,* AL RASCHOUN *leading.* ALI BABA *comes out from behind the rock* R. *mopping his brow.*)

ALI BABA. Phew! That was a close shave! (*He approaches the cave, staring at it.*) I wonder if I dare go in? All the riches of Persia are there! Selima and I could be made as wealthy as Cassim—more so! With all that booty, what could I not do? Dare I? How long will Kemal be? He would say "No!" Or would he? I wonder! I'll risk it! (*He goes yet nearer, and then speaks in a hoarse whisper.*) Open—Sesame!

(*The stone rolls back.* ALI BABA *staggers back, then approaches stealthily. The sound of horses is heard again, dying away.* ALI BABA *waits, then creeps into the cave, and whispers loudly.*)

Shut—Sesame!

(*The stone rolls over the mouth of the cave.* ALI BABA *is hidden.* KEMAL *enters hurriedly* L.)

KEMAL. Father! Father, where are you? Father! (*He moves about, looking behind the rock* R., *then comes to* C.) Gone! What if the robbers found him—killed him? O father, my father! How can I go back to Selima my mother and say I did not protect you? Father! Father!

ALI BABA (*within the cave*). Open, Sesame!

(KEMAL *staggers back down* R.C. *The stone rolls away and* ALI BABA *emerges, laden with jewels, boxes and silks.*)

KEMAL. Father! You are safe!

ALI BABA. Yes, Kemal, my son! Safe! And rich! I learned the secret of opening the robbers' cave wherein their booty is hid!

KEMAL. Oh, my father!

ALI BABA. Fetch the camel, my son. No! Help me to carry this out to the camel. Our camel-driving days are over!

KEMAL. But all this is not ours!

ALI BABA. It is more ours than theirs. And we shall not forget the poor now we are rich. We, who have known poverty, will pity and relieve the poverty of others.

KEMAL. I can hardly believe it! It's like a dream!

ALI BABA. So I thought. But see, it's real—all real . . .

(*He fingers the booty and pours out coins from the bags.*)

KEMAL. And do we leave the cave open?

ALI BABA. No, we will close it—for the last time—and then, to Baghdad!

(*He turns slowly and faces the cave.* KEMAL *watches.*)

SHUT, SESAME!

(*The stone rolls over the mouth of the cave.*)

Never more. Never more will I enter. I am satisfied.

KEMAL. Let us go, my father.

ALI BABA. Yes, let us go.

(*They stand a moment, watching the mouth of the cave. Soft Eastern music. The light fades, leaving only a gold spot of light on the stone. Quietly, they exit* L. *carrying the booty.*)

The TABS *close.*

During the Scene Change:

March cross-over of ROBBERS, *with chorus. This is followed by entrance of* MORGIANA, *who sings a reprise of No.* 4, *and finishes this with an Oriental Dance.*

The TABS *open.*

Scene 3.

Scene.—*The Bazaar, as before. Early Evening. The stage is filled with slaves, moving and talking excitedly. There is a background of music. A shout, as a fantastically dressed black slave leaps into the scene, and flings a shower of gold to the others. He goes into a wild, short dance. Then,* R., Morgiana *enters. She dances gracefully, and then, joined by the black slave, they do a wilder dance.* (A Chorus *for the Slaves may be added, or blended into this.*) *All exeunt.* Gogetti *and* Rosetti *enter at once* L.)

Rosetti. Oh, look! Here they come! Those boys! The fishmonger and the greengrocer!
Gogetti. How common! Let's pretend we haven't seen them.

(*They stroll about nonchalantly arm in arm. Enter* Mustapha Nutha *and* Mustapha Dubbuhl *singing raucously. They see the girls and suddenly stop and go coy. Dithering business as they approach.*)

Nutha. Do you see what I see, O Mustapha Dubbuhl?
Dubbuhl (*covering his eyes and uncovering them again quickly*). Yes, if you see what I see, O Mustapha Nutha.
Gogetti (*with elaborate unconcern*). Terrible weather we're having, isn't it?
Rosetti (*equally unconcerned*). Yes, *so* bad for the crops.
Dubbuhl (*loudly*). Good for fishing though, isn't it?
Nutha (*sniggering*). And for picking passion fruit!
Gogetti. I always say one never *quaite* knows what to wear.

(Mustapha Nutha *and* Mustapha Dubbuhl *are both swaggering along a few paces behind the girls, who suddenly turn and come face to face with them and pretend great surprise and shyness.*)

Gogetti (*in a faint voice*). Oh!
Rosetti. Oh!

(*They both look at the ground intently.* NUTHA *and* DUBBUHL *look puzzled and get down on their knees to see what they are looking at.*)

NUTHA. I can't see what they've dropped, can you, Dubbuhl?

DUBBUHL. They both dropped their eyes a moment ago, that's all I saw.

(*They both stand up again.*)

NUTHA (*looking at the girls' frigid attitude*). I think the temperature's dropped as well! (*Shivers ostentatiously.*)

DUBBUHL (*to* GOGETTI *as she raises her eyes a little*). Er—good morning, Mam'selle Gogetti. I trust the cod's head boiled well?

GOGETTI. Yes, and all the time I watched it boil I could not help thinking . . .

DUBBUHL. Yes?

GOGETTI. . . . of you!

(*The girls laugh.* MUSTAPHA DUBBUHL *recoils.*)

NUTHA (*to* DUBBUHL). Let me try—let *me* try! (*To* ROSETTI.) And how is my little peach blossom this morning?

ROSETTI. Much better than your cabbages, Mustapha Nutha. You see, *my* heart is *whole*.

DUBBUHL (*delightedly*). He's had it! He's had it!

(*He goes aside and confers with* MUSTAPHA NUTHA *for a moment. They both whisper and gesticulate. The girls stand still and pat their hair, smiling mischievously at each other.*)

DUBBUHL (*approaching the girls again*). Er—doing anything tonight?

NUTHA. How about seeing a little snake charming with us?

ROSETTI. A snake? Charming with *you*?

GOGETTI. The only animal that would be!

(MUSTAPHA NUTHA *and* MUSTAPHA DUBBUHL *collapse.*)

No. 7. SCENA : *Chant and Dance*. (SNAKE CHARMER *and*
CHORUS).

(*Enter the full* CHORUS *of* TRADERS, CROWD, SLAVES, *etc.,
with a very ancient* SNAKE CHARMER *in their midst. He
takes his place* C. *and sits cross-legged in front of a large box,
the others grouped about him. He begins to chant an
Eastern song. The lights dim, and gradually a snake's
head emerges from the box, rising higher as the chanting
goes on to a pitch of frenzy.* ROSETTI *and* GOGETTI
clutch MUSTAPHA NUTHA *and* MUSTAPHA DUBBUHL,
afraid. The CROWD *join in the song, and engage in a wild
kind of dance, until the* SNAKE CHARMER *slowly induces
the snake to return to the box. The* CROWD *shout their
approval of the act, and some throw coins to the* CHARMER.
He goes out L.C. *followed by the* CROWD R. *and* L. *with*
ROSETTI, GOGETTI, MUSTAPHA NUTHA *and* MUSTAPHA
DUBBUHL *bringing up the rear. Enter* ALI BABA *and*
KEMAL, *carrying the treasure.* ALI BABA *kneels on the
floor and opens his red handkerchief, revealing glittering
jewels, gold and silver. He empties the contents of his
pockets on top of this and makes a pile of his booty, then
stands up and surveys it with rather a bewildered smile.*)

ALI BABA (*looking round and shouting*). Selima ! Morgiana ! Come and see what we have brought you !

(SELIMA *and* MORGIANA *enter from the house.*)

SELIMA (*aghast*). Ali Baba ! My lord ! What is this ?
MORGIANA. Oh, my master !
SELIMA (*very excited*). Ali ! Where did you get so much treasure ?

(MORGIANA *moves a little nearer to* KEMAL, *behind* SELIMA
and ALI BABA.)

ALI BABA. I met a band of robbers in the forest and watched them hide their booty. When they had gone, well —I just helped myself.
MORGIANA (*drawing back afraid*). Oh, my lord, I am afraid for you ! The robbers will have their revenge.

KEMAL. Nonsense, Morgiana, how will they know? We shall all be rich now. There will be no more need for us to go leading camels across the desert.

SELIMA (*clasping her hands delightedly*). Oh, we shall be richer than your brother Cassim and that proud wife of his!

ALI BABA. Wait a moment, not quite so fast, my dear. We don't know how rich we are till we have measured the gold.

KEMAL. Uncle Cassim has a measure. Shall I go and borrow that, father?

ALI BABA. Yes, but be sure not to say *why* I want it. Let Morgiana go.

KEMAL. I'll go with her, in case they won't let her have it. Come, Morgiana.

MORGIANA (*anxiously as they move* R.). I do not like it. No good will come of it.

(*They exeunt* R.)

SELIMA (*looking worried*). O my lord, are you sure that all is right? The robbers will not find you, will they?

ALI BABA (*laughing and patting her on the shoulder*). Of course not, O Turtle Dove of Tremendous Timidity! They had no idea anyone saw them. Listen! We saw them approach. I sent Kemal to hide the camel, and I concealed myself behind a rock. I watched, and the robbers, using a secret password, opened the cave without hands!

SELIMA. Without hands?

ALI BABA. The stone over the cave rolled back when they said " Open, Sesame! " I waited, while they stacked within it their latest booty and came out again. Then, after a most ribald and shameless song, they rode off, and I, I alone, O Flower of Most Commendable Credulity, opened the cave by the same means, er—furnished myself with an adequate reward for my patience and—er—courage, and emerged, laden. Finally (*with a fine air of casual vanity*) we just—closed the cave again, and came home. Just—closed the cave—quite simple!

SELIMA. But how?

ALI BABA (*airily*). Oh—merely cried " Shut Sesame " !
SELIMA. Really ! (*Significantly.*) Very simple indeed—said like that.
ALI. Surely, O Pomegranate of Paralysing Perspicacity, you believe me ?
SELIMA. I hope, O Partner of Perpetual Peregrinations, you will never give me cause *not* to.
ALI BABA (*doubtfully*). Oh.

(*Enter* KEMAL, *followed by* MORGIANA. *He carries a pair of scales, which he gives to* ALI.)

KEMAL. I've got them ! Aunt Nella was, to say the least, reluctant and suspicious ! She wanted to know a great deal, but I fear I disappointed her !
SELIMA. The nosey old . . .
ALI. Ah—ah—ah ! Let us weigh the gold, and forget her ! Weigh the gold ! Kemal, set out the pearls, the gems ! Selima, hold the scales while I fill them—high—with gold—precious gold ! Morgiana—(*he looks at her*)—our little Morgiana looks sad—give her some gem, Selima, to brighten her . . . (*During this he is filling the scales.*)
MORGIANA. The love of money is a terrible thing, O my master.
ALI. The lack of it, Morgiana, is not amusing ! (*Awestricken, as he examines the scales.*) Allah ! This way we shall be even richer than my skinflint brother Cassim !
SELIMA (*as they empty the scales and refill it*). It can't be true ! It's like a dream . . .
KEMAL. It *is* true, mother, and after today . . .
ALI (*with rising excitement*). After today she shall be like the most favoured wife of the Caliph—the Red Rose of the Harem ! The . . .
SELIMA. That is enough, Ali ! I am not sure your comparisons are complimentary !
ALI. They are, I assure you ! And Kemal shall have an honoured position in the town as son of its most wealthy citizen ! We will have slaves—and Morgiana shall be appointed over them all ! (*Raising a jewelled cup as if about to drink a toast.*) Here's to the House of Ali Baba !

KEMAL (*with a wink at* MORGIANA). May Allah protect it and prosper its fortunes!

ALI (*rising*). Away! Bring the treasure! Within the house we'll store it! Bring all—Selima—Kemal!

(*They rise, and gather everything up and hurry to the house.*)

SELIMA. Leave nothing, Kemal! Open the door, Morgiana, my hands are full!

(*They exeunt into the house, but leave the scales on the ground. Enter* NELLA *and* CASSIM, R.)

NELLA (*talking as they cross to* L.C.). And Kemal came to borrow the scales—why? Why? I could find out nothing! But . . . (*She pokes* CASSIM *in the ribs.*)

CASSIM. But? (*With a knowing grin.*) Aha! I guarantee you devised some scheme for learning their secret!

NELLA. Ye-es, indeed! I put a little soft tallow in the pans of the scales, so that some of whatever they measured in them would stick!

CASSIM (*admiringly*). O Soul of Surreptitious Sagacity! It would take more than my simple brother to outwit you!

NELLA (*seeing the scales*). Cassim! The scales! Look! (*She picks them up and examines them.*) Gold! Gold! (*They both examine their find.*) Gold has been weighed in them!

CASSIM. Gold in truth! You're right, O Spouse of Secrecy and Sinister Solicitude! Gold—in the hands of Ali, my Brother of Ignominious Impecuniosity! Somehow or other my brother has seized a quantity of gold! I wonder where, O Companion of Characteristic Curiosity?

NELLA. We must find out, Cassim! Question him! Trap him into admission!

CASSIM. Better still to flatter and fawn on him!

NELLA. We will call on him! You deal with him, and I with Selima! Knock at the door, Cassim! Knock at the door, O thou Personification of Procrastination!

CASSIM. I will! Trust me—(*going up and knocking at* ALI'S *door*). Trust me to ferret out the source of his fortune!

(*The door opens.* ALI *appears, and moves out, as* SELIMA, KEMAL *and* MORGIANA *group behind him.*)

Good morrow, brother. You look well. Selima, I trust is well—and Kemal well?

ALI (*who is holding a gold ornament in one hand and a gold cup in the other*). Well—well—well! And I hope you are!

CASSIM. Indeed! Indeed! I thank you! I see you have struck gold in your camel-driving today? May we—(*suavely*) enquire? Or is it a great secret, O Brother of Ostensible Opulence?

ALI BABA (*happily*). Oh, no, it is no secret, Cassim. Listen, and I'll tell you the tale of the Magic Cave. . . .

(MORGIANA *makes a movement as if to stop him, but* KEMAL *gently restrains her.*)

. . . and what is more, though you have no ear for music, I insist on recounting it to you in song, O my Relative of Monumental Materialism!

No. 8. " OPEN SESAME "! .. .. (ALI BABA).
(*Air : The Poacher "—Traditional.*)

ALI BABA. I rested by a stony cave upon the desert way
When Forty Robbers came in sight, I hid myself away,
The secret of their golden hoard they soon revealed to me—
FOR—the words to roll the stone away were " Open, Sesame."

ALL (*each in character*).
FOR—the words to roll the stone away,
Were " Open Sesame "!

ALI BABA (*as they all draw nearer*).
The Robbers gone—as sly as sly I crept towards the store
For I was rather short of cash and badly needed more!
Oh, what a bold adventurer is Yours so faithfullee—

FOR—I smoothly rolled the stone away with
"Open Sesame"!
ALL (*as before*).
AH!—he smoothly rolled the stone away
With "Open Sesame"!
ALI BABA. I entered in and took my fill, delighted with
my quest,
So now I'm fairly affluent, and mean to take
a rest.
To camel-driving I can say "O Pish!" and
"Fiddle-de-dee"
AND—all because I knew the words were
"Open Sesame"!
ALL. AND—all because he knew the words were
"Open Sesame."

(*The* BABAS *go into a burlesque stately dance,* CASSIM *partners* SELIMA, ALI *partners* NELLA, *and* KEMAL *dances with* MORGIANA. *During the last repeat line, the* CROWD *have been returning. They stare, open-mouthed, at the friendly atmosphere in the Baba family.*)

CROWD (*singing*).

The Baba tribe appear to be on most delightful terms
Though normally they look upon each other just as
worms,
We wonder at the origin of this fraternity!
THE BABAS. O-OH! It's all because we know the word
is "Open Sesame"!
CROWD. WHAT a great relief it is to know it's
"Open Sesame"!

They break into a lively dance as

The CURTAIN *falls.*

(NOTE: *The above Number must be sung in a rather burlesque fashion. The first word of each last line should be fortissimo and sustained.*)

ACT II.

Scene 1.

Scene.—*The desert valley and cave as in Act I.*
It is night.

When the Curtain *rises it is quite dark. Then, as moonlight fades in on the skycloth the* Desert Spirits *are seen on the ridge, in silhouette. There is soft music (Suggested music, " The Funeral March of a Marionette ") and the* Spirits *perform a* Ballet, *being joined by other* Spirits, *emerging from behind the palms and rocks on stage level, lit by moonlight.*

No. 9.   Dance of the Desert Spirits   ..   (Dancers.)

(*As the* Ballet *ends, the* Spirits *on stage level exeunt, and then only the lighting on the sky-cloth remains, and the* Spirits *on the ridge are once more posed in silhouette. Then, as if a cloud has passed over the moon, darkness falls, and when the light fades in again, the* Spirits *are gone, but* Cassim *is standing at down* R.C. *facing the cave.*)

Cassim. This *must* be it! The rock exactly as my brother Ali described it—the cave with doors that open at a word! Oh, how I long to feel my hands upon those jewels . . . The gold! (*He chuckles and advances slowly towards the cave.*) Now to test my brother's tale—if he has spoken the truth, all, all is mine! (*He raises a skinny hand towards the cave, and calls.*) Open, Sesame!

(*The stone rolls open, and* Cassim *gasps and staggers back, amazed.*)

Ah! (*He enters the mouth of the cave and gazes at the treasure.*) Oh—riches—fabulous—unbelievable! Never had I dreamed of bounty such as this! Such treasure—*mine*! *All* mine . . . All mine! (*He turns.*) Now must I shut myself within, that no one else may know the secret. (*Lifting his eyes to the roof of the cave.*) Shut, O Sesame!

(*He withdraws a pace as the stone closes and hides him. There are a few bars of the Ballet Music, and some of the* SPIRITS *appear on the ridge above the cave, pose, and make doomful gestures towards the doors. The wind wails, horses' hooves are heard. The* SPIRITS *exeunt and Music dies away. The moonlight becomes a little brighter.* SMASHEM *enters* R. *followed by* GRABBEM.)

SMASHEM (*after looking round*). No one here! Not a soul!
GRABBEM. Not a sausage!
SMASHEM. Did you expect to find a sausage?
GRABBEM. No, but I could do with one.
SMASHEM. That's right! Always thinking of your stomach!
GRABBEM. Well, it's always reminding me!
SMASHEM. The point is—who is the owner of those twelve white mules out there? Has our master—er—" borrowed " any white mules lately?
BOTH. No!
SMASHEM. Have we—brave as we are—captured single-handed twelve beautiful white mules?
BOTH. No!
SMASHEM. YES!
GRABBEM. Oh—when?
SMASHEM. When would *you* say?
GRABBEM. Oh, any old time—any old time—what are you talking about?
SMASHEM. Listen! (*He clutches* GRABBEM'S *arm.*) When our master Al Raschoun arrives, we will describe, with lurid details, how we fought fifty armed merchants, slew them with exceeding slaughter, and made off, laughing . . . (*he gives a long melodramatic laugh*) laughing—like that, with no less than twelve beautiful white mules and all accoutrements. Alone we did it!
GRABBEM. And will he believe us?
BOTH. No!

(*They both shake hands violently, and then spring apart as a shout and peal of triumphant laughter is heard from within the cave.* SMASHEM *and* GRABBEM *rush down* L. *in terror and turn to gaze at the cave. Another shout, laughter and noise of heavy objects being moved about.*)

SMASHEM. There is someone within!
GRABBEM (*seizing* SMASHEM *and shuddering*). Don't leave me! Don't leave me!
SMASHEM. Coward!
GRABBEM. Who's a coward?
SMASHEM. You are!
GRABBEM. I am?
SMASHEM. I am!
GRABBEM. You are?
SMASHEM. Both of us—stop arguing—there he is again!

(*They listen. Noises repeated.*)

GRABBEM (*with pretended relish*). Shall we—shall we go inside and bring him out, and carve him up in little pieces and get a reward from our master? Shee-all weee?
SMASHEM. No-oo, weee wo-won't!
GRABBEM. And whyee no-not?
SMASHEM. Because—we aren't allowed to use THE WORD except in our master's presence.
GRABBEM. So we aren't! I'm rather glad, aren't you?
SMASHEM. Oh, I yam-I-yam-I-yam-I-yam!
GRABBEM. Look! Here comes our master! Hola!
SMASHEM. Huroo!

(*A clatter of hooves, and* AL RASCHOUN *enters with the* ROBBERS.)

RASCHOUN. Aha! I see you are working better, boys! All praise to you for capturing those fine twelve white mules I see tethered without. And single-handed, too. Well done!

(*A pause.* SMASHEM *and* GRABBEM *look at each other, incredulously, grin, and then turn to* AL RASCHOUN, *holding out their hands.*)

Sc. 1]   ALI BABA   31

SMASHEM } (together). { Thank you very much. We never thought it would come off. As a matter of fact . . .
GRABBEM }

RASCHOUN. Go on.
SMASHEM. Having fought and slain fifty armed merchants . . .
GRABBEM. Single-handed . . .
SMASHEM. And brought twelve fine white mules to our meeting place—(*aside to* GRABBEM) we're doing well, we're doing well! (*To* AL RASCHOUN) we found one merchant had escaped and—er—er . . .
GRABBEM. He—well—er . . . (*They point to the cave.*)
RASCHOUN. Out with it, before I have you buried head downward in the sand.
SMASHEM. You tell him—I haven't had my Bemax.
GRABBEM. We have a visitor within.
RASCHOUN. Within?
GRABBEM. Within the cave!
(AL RASCHOUN *gives a shout. All turn to the cave.*)
SMASHEM. Listen!

(*Noises in the cave.*)

CASSIM (*within*). Open, O Sesame!

(*All stagger back as the stone rolls aside. No one is seen.*)

RASCHOUN. Come forth, O honoured and unexpected guest!

(*No one appears.* AL RASCHOUN *gestures to* SMASHEM *and* GRABBEM.)

Bring him out.
ROBBERS (*shouting ad. lib.*). Bring him out! Kill him! Slay him!
RASCHOUN. Silence all!

(*He gestures.* SMASHEM *and* GRABBEM, *trembling, knock against each other, enter the cave. They emerge, with* CASSIM *between them. Shouts and murmurs from the* ROBBERS.)

RASCHOUN (*bowing*). Ah! Thrice welcome is the unexpected guest! Your name?

(CASSIM *hesitates*.)

Your name!

CASSIM (*cunningly*). Benoudah Khan, of Mukka-dan.

RASCHOUN. How knew you of the cave and of the word —the magic word?

CASSIM. I read it in a book of tales . . .

(AL RASCHOUN'S *hand goes to his dagger*.)

(*Throwing himself on his knees*.) Oh, kill me not! Spare me! I meant no harm!

RASCHOUN. Rise, Lord Benoudah Khan of Mukka-dan! An honoured visitor! (*To the others*.) Give me wine! Two cups!

(CASSIM *rises, wondering*. AL RASCHOUN *turns and takes a bottle of wine which is handed to him and pours two cups, which are held out by a* ROBBER. *Unseen by* CASSIM, *he pours a powder into one, and leers at the others*.)

Come! Drink with Al Raschoun and join our company! A welcome new companion!

(*He raises his cup and drinks*. CASSIM *does also, and immediately falls to the ground*. AL RASCHOUN, *with a shout of rage, flings his cup down*.)

Take him—throw him within the cave!

A ROBBER. Is he dead, O master?

RASCHOUN. He has but an hour or two to live. Take him away!

(SMASHEM *and* GRABBEM *fling* CASSIM *into the cave*.)

Shut Sesame!

(*The stone closes*.)

We must away! Mukka-dan! Ha! This man's from Baghdad, or my name is not Raschoun! To Baghdad, then!

Sc. 1] ALI BABA 33

ROBBERS (*as they go*). To Baghdad! To Baghdad!

(*They exeunt.* AL RASCHOUN *strides after them.*)

GRABBEM (*to* SMASHEM). To Baghdad! Come on now, bring your bag, dad!
RASCHOUN (*off*). Follow me! And bring the mules.
SMASHEM. What—us?
GRABBEM. Yus! Us!
SMASHEM. Oh, I do hate mules. They're so *obstinate*!

(*They exeunt. The* SPIRITS *enter. Short dance and exeunt.*
ALI BABA *enters* L. MORGIANA *follows him on. The light of dawn begins to glow in the sky.*)

ALI BABA. This is the place, Morgiana. I would have you see that it is as I said.
MORGIANA. It is an evil place, my master.
ALI BABA. Nonsense! Though I said I was satisfied, I am tempted.
MORGIANA. Oh, master!
ALI BABA. We just have time to seize another bag of gold—a roll of silk for Selima and some trinkets for yourself.
MORGIANA. No! I wear nothing that is hidden here.
ALI BABA. Oh—really? Well, do as you please! Watch now! (*He calls.*) Open, Sesame!

(*The stone rolls back. He enters. Another moment and he gives a great cry and reappears.*)

ALI BABA. My brother Cassim!
MORGIANA. Has he been here, too, master, and stolen all?
ALI BABA. He lies there—dead! Killed by the robbers! (*He covers his head with his hands.*)
MORGIANA. Did I not say it was an evil place and that no good would come of stealing plunder, master? (*She kneels at his feet.*) O master,! Master! It might have been you—you, to be killed! (*She shudders and bows her head.*)

ALI BABA (*touched*). Why, Morgiana, would you have cared so much?

MORGIANA (*simply*). Master, I live only to serve you—and yours.

ALI BABA. You are a good girl, Morgiana. Indeed, I almost look on you as one of my family . . .

MORGIANA. O my lord—if you but meant that. (*With a little gesture of pleading.*) If you but thought of me as one of you—as—as a daughter . . .

ALI BABA. Come, come, we are forgetting poor Cassim. He lies there, on a litter. We must carry him out, place him upon the camel's back and take him home.

(*He goes sadly into the cave.* MORGIANA *follows. The* DESERT SPIRITS *appear on the ridge, to Music as before, and dance. To the music,* ALI BABA *and* MORGIANA *reappear, with* CASSIM *on the litter and begin to move to the* L. *exit, as the lighting fades.*)

The TABS *close.*

During the Scene change:

The DESERT SPIRITS *do a dance in front of the* TABS, *and exeunt. This is followed by* ALI, MORGIANA, *and the litter with* CASSIM *on it. They cross over to the music. After exeunt, there is Introductory Music to the next scene.*

The TABS *open.*

Scene 2.

Scene.—*The Street of the Bazaars, as in Act I.*

When the Curtain *rises the traders are at their stalls. A number of people are moving from one stall to the other making purchases, humming the refrain of the opening number, with a good deal of pantomime and business of animated conversation. The humming dies down as* Heelam, *busy at his work, sings.*

No. 10. Song: " Secrets " .. (Heelam *and* Crowd.)
(*Air :* " *Tobacco is an Indian weed.*")

Heelam. I sit so patiently all day
And just to while the hours away
As folks go by
On them I spy
I'm a devil to revel in secrets !
Crowd. He's a devil to revel in secrets !
Heelam. Sometimes I hear perchance a lad
Breathe words of love to maiden glad
He steals a kiss
I watch her bliss—
I'm a devil to revel in secrets !
Crowd. He's a devil to revel in secrets !
Heelam. I've watched old Cassim steal away
To get a little change each day
From Nella's charms
To " The Caliph's Arms "
I'm a devil and revel in secrets !
Crowd. He's a devil !
Such a devil !
He's a devil to revel in secrets !
Chorus. We guess the baker uses bran
We know our sugar's mainly sand
But Dubbuhl's dish
Of week-old fish
He cannot keep a secret !
He'll never !
No, he'll never !
He'll never keep a secret !

(*The* CHORUS *sing the repeat refrain, and during this, various* ROBBERS *mingle with the crowd. They are seen to ask many questions and receive in reply mainly shakes of the head and negative gestures. The* CHORUS *and the* ROBBERS *begin to exeunt in ones and twos.* ALI BABA *comes out of his house, hesitates, and then moves* R. *as he sees* KEMAL *enter up* R. *The following dialogue is spoken to a soft background of music.*)

KEMAL. How is Uncle Cassim?
ALI BABA. Sh-sh! He still lives. I dare not call a physician in case questions are asked. Until he is safe in his own house the Robbers must think he is dead.
KEMAL. There were some evil characters in the crowd just now. I think they might have been robbers in search of uncle.
ALI BABA. I am sure of it. If we can spread abroad the news of a mysterious death they may be satisfied and forget about it. But how are we to do it?
KEMAL. I think Morgiana has an idea. She is being very mysterious.

(MORGIANA, *dressed in a long black robe, and veiled, comes down the street* R. *and joins them on their* R., *at first not seen by them.*)

ALI BABA. But what can *she* do?
MORGIANA (*as she joins them*). Ah, what can she *not* do, my master?
ALI BABA. Who are you?
MORGIANA. Ah, my disguise is better than I thought! You did not know your humble slave, Morgiana! (*She unveils.*)
KEMAL. Morgiana!
MORGIANA. Sh-sh! Come with me—but do not let us be seen by Heelam! (*They withdraw up* R. *by the corner of the Bazaar.*) Kemal, you must go up that street, and stay away for a while. You, master (*to* ALI BABA) must go back to the house, not by the front door, but by the back. Then—leave all to me. Quickly, master!
ALI BABA. I will do as you say, but . . .

MORGIANA. Quickly!

(ALI BABA *hurries away and off* R.)

Now you, Kemal.
KEMAL. One kiss!
MORGIANA. No!
KEMAL. Morgiana!
MORGIANA. I say, no! For one thing, there is no time—I say, go!
KEMAL (*humbly*). Yes, Morgiana.

(*He exits down* R. MORGIANA *waits a moment, watching* HEELAM, *who begins to sing again. Then* MORGIANA *goes with slow, stealthy steps towards him.*)

MORGIANA. You are happy, master.
HEELAM (*stopping in his singing and turning to her*). Why should I not be?
MORGIANA. No reason. But would you not pity a young widow?
HEELAM. If she is as pretty as you I would rather *console* her. Your husband is dead?
MORGIANA. Yes.
HEELAM. You do not look sorrowful. Was he young?
MORGIANA. No, old. Old and mean. And I do not wish his brother to know he is dead, or he will take all his money.
HEELAM. I see! Well, as you were not fond of your husband and are pretty, and he is rich and dead, I am very interested.
MORGIANA. You would—console me?
HEELAM. Delighted!
MORGIANA. Well, first come and sew his shroud for me.
HEELAM. And then?
MORGIANA. We shall see!

(HEELAM *rises.*)

But first, I must bind your eyes, because you must not be able to tell anyone where I live—yet.

(*She takes a black scarf from her dress.*)

HEELAM. I usually go into these things with my eyes open, but, well, anything for a change.

MORGIANA. Here, then. (*She binds his eyes and turns him round three times.*)

HEELAM. I am feeling giddy, but whether that is going round and round or whether it is the thought of your beauty, I am not sure.

MORGIANA. Undoubtedly my beauty. Come with me. (*She leads him* L. *then back up* R., *turns him again and finally takes him into* ALI BABA'S *house.*)

(*Enter* SMASHEM *and* GRABBEM *up* R.)

GRABBEM (*as they come down*). You're a fine spy, you are. All day you've been at this job and found out nothing.

SMASHEM. Have you found out anything?

GRABBEM. Certainly.

SMASHEM. What?

GRABBEM. That somebody in this town has suddenly become very rich and has bought a big house.

SMASHEM. Who is it?

GRABBEM. I haven't the least idea. Still, it's something.

SMASHEM. You tell Al Raschoun that, and see what he says.

GRABBEM. Well, he swallowed the yarn about the fifty merchants and the mules! Let's think something up.

SMASHEM. Think? Are you going to *think*?

GRABBEM. Naturally.

SMASHEM. What with?

GRABBEM. Something you've never heard of—my brains.

SMASHEM. No, I've never heard of them. Have you had them long? Do introduce me.

GRABBEM. My brains, let me tell you, are very particular who they are introduced to.

SMASHEM. Mine are very exclusive too. Upstage—oh, very, very upstage!

GRABBEM. H'm! We both seem to have exceptional intellects.

Sc. 2]   ALI BABA   39

SMASHEM. What a comfort! What a comfort!

No. 11. DUET, "Brains" .. (SMASHEM *and* GRABBEM.)
(*Air* : "*Here's to the Maiden of Bashful Fifteen.*")

SMASHEM. I have a brain, it is perfectly plain
              The only one to rely on.
GRABBEM. I have a mind that is always behind
              You can use it with pleasure to try on!
BOTH.   Oh, for a tale!
              Think up a tale,
SMASHEM. It has to be good for a ready cash sale!

(*They shake hands.*)

SMASHEM. Wonderful brain! It has started a train
              Of notions I cannot remember!
GRABBEM. Intellect fine! It's a positive mine . . .

(*He pauses.* SMASHEM *regards him pitifully, then advances, rolling up his sleeves.*)

              Tumpety-tum—in September!
SMASHEM (*spoken*). What do you mean? "Tumpety-tum in September"?
GRABBEM. Don't you like it?
SMASHEM. It doesn't mean anything.
GRABBEM. Oh, that's all right, old boy! It's just to fit in with "notions I cannot remember"!
SMASHEM. We'll try again.

(*They sing.*)

BOTH.   Oh for a scheme
              Think up a scheme
              To keep Al Raschoun from blowing off
                steam!

(*They shake hands.*)

GRABBEM. Another spasm!
SMASHEM. Craniums full as ours give a pull
              In circles where brain is respected!

GRABBEM. Cerebral force as a matter of course
In the criminal world is expected!
SMASHEM. Sell him a pup!
GRABBEM. I give it up!

(GRABBEM *looks nervously at* SMASHEM, *gulps, and then sings.*)

Tumpetty-tumpetty—Up for the Cup!
SMASHEM. " Tumpetty-tumpetty! I tell you it means NOTHING AT ALL!

(GRABBEM *flinches and backs away.*)

And " Up for the Cup " is ridiculous!
GRABBEM. Ah, but thousands of people do it—now the year Aston Villa beat . . .
SMASHEM. Grabbem! How can you? How can you mention *football* in the middle of a crisis!
GRABBEM (*after a pause and business; to the audience*). Ladies and gentlemen—I apologise to the government!
SMASHEM (*to the conductor of the orchestra*). Another basinful of music, please, Mr. Penniwistle.
CONDUCTOR. Mr. Smashem, my name is *not* Penniwistle!
SMASHEM (*if* CONDUCTOR *is thin*). Well, you look like one, anyway!
(*if* CONDUCTOR *is stout*). You don't look like one, either! What *is* your name?
CONDUCTOR. My name is Tim.
GRABBEM. Oh, of *course*! Tim Pani! (*Pointing to end of orchestra well.*) But shouldn't you be down the other end? (*Business of imitating playing tympani.*) Bom-bom-beddy bom-bom!
CONDUCTOR. Shall we proceed?
SMASHEM } (*together*). Delighted!
GRABBEM

SMASHEM (*pointing to someone in the audience*).
Girl over there with the lovely red (fair or dark) hair.
I wonder if she could assist us!
GRABBEM (*to* SMASHEM).
Yes, I believe—if her husband would leave—
She isn't the kind to resist us!

SMASHEM (*to the* AUDIENCE).
Just let us know!
GRABBEM.   After the show!
SMASHEM.   Just ask for Smashem
GRABBEM.   And Grabbem
BOTH.   And CO!

(*Dance. Enter* AL RASCHOUN *and four of the* ROBBERS.)

RASCHOUN (*who is in a rage*). Pah! You pretty posse of petty pilferers! To come and tell me such a thing! To have let the magic cave be plundered yet again and the body of that thieving merchant be stolen! At this rate we'll be bankrupt in a week. You're only fit to be baby watchers—and then you'd let them steal each other's dummies! I warn you, fail me once more and I'll cut you up in little pieces!
    SMASHEM. Quite little pieces?
    RASCHOUN. Into thin slices. (*With mincing and descriptive gestures.*)
    GRABBEM. Oh, goody-goody-GOODY!
    SMASHEM. I'm such a one for thin slices!
    RASCHOUN. And thrown to the vultures!
    SMASHEM } (*together*). { Here we are! Here we are!
    GRABBEM }   { Here we are!

(*Business of going round and distributing fish to seals at the Zoo.*)

Next feeding time at four o'clock! Pass along to the reptiles, please. And keep to the left. Monkey nuts, bath buns—tuppence a bag.

    (*They catch* AL RASCHOUN'S *eyes and desist.*)

RASCHOUN. For the last time, are you or are you not going to find this thief—or his family—and where he has hidden our plunder?
    ROBBERS (*one by one, sadly holding up their hands*). Aye! Aye! Aye! Aye! (*Etc.*)
    SMASHEM } (*together*). Us, too!
    GRABBEM }

ROBBERS (*one by one, very languidly*). Death to the robber! Let's kill him! We'll be revenged! He must die!
SMASHEM }
GRABBEM } (*together*). He's a naughty BOY!
RASCHOUN. Go! All of you, before I LOSE MY TEMPER!

(*They all scuttle off.* AL RASCHOUN *paces about for a moment, then stops as* HEELAM *enters up* L. *He is still blindfolded. He stops by his stall and then takes off the bandage and sees* AL RASCHOUN *watching him.*)

RASCHOUN. Good afternoon—or rather, evening.
HEELAM. Sandals to mend?
RASCHOUN. No. May I ask why you walk the street blindfolded?
HEELAM. I've been sewing a shroud for a funeral. Oh, very jolly!
RASCHOUN. Ah, indeed? Blindfold?
HEELAM. Oh, I can do anything blindfold. Tomorrow I shall be consoling the widow.
RASCHOUN. Blindfold?
HEELAM. No, but she made it a condition that I should not see where she lived, because she did not want her late husband's brother to know until she had possession of her legacy.
RASCHOUN. Tell me more. You do not know which house?
HEELAM (*pointing to* ALI BABA'S *house*). Something tells me it was that one. And yet something tells me it can't be, because that is the house of Ali Baba, a poor cameldriver who has suddenly and mysteriously become very rich. I can say no more, as I am hoping to console the widow.
RASCHOUN. An interesting story. (*Giving him money.*) Drink my health at yonder tavern, for entertaining me.
HEELAM. I don't usually get money for nothing—but, well, anything for a change. Good evening.

(*He exits* L. AL RASCHOUN *goes to* HEELAM'S *stall, takes a piece of chalk and marks a large cross on* ALI BABA'S *door. He then crosses* R.)

RASCHOUN. Saved by a talkative cobbler and a piece of chalk! Smashem! Grabbem! Where are you, you lazy louts? Come here!

(*He exits up* R. MORGIANA *comes down in a panic. She sees the cross, gets the chalk from* HEELAM'S *stall and marks a cross on every door. No sooner has she done this than* KEMAL *enters down* R.)

KEMAL. Morgiana!
MORGIANA. Kemal! O my lord Kemal! (*She goes to him.*)
KEMAL. Oh, Morgiana, don't "my lord" me any more . . . (*He tries to take her in his arms.*)
MORGIANA. I may love you but you are still my lord. But listen! I succeeded in getting Heelam the cobbler to sew up the shroud of a dummy I made, so the news should get about that a mysterious death has occurred. But afterwards, I heard him tell a very evil-looking man who I feel sure is the chief robber your father told us he saw at the cave. In fact, he marked your door with a cross so that he may know which house to return to. Look, I have made a cross on every other house to confuse him.
KEMAL. Morgiana, how clever of you! What do we do now?
MORGIANA. Now is the time for you to act. Your Uncle Cassim is now stirring—the medicine we gave him has saved him. Tonight you must bury the dummy, and take Cassim in secret to your new home. But you must not come back here. We must all go to this new house your father has bought, taking the treasure, and leaving this house quite empty. Your father is now inside, packing everything in readiness. It is already night. We must make haste.
KEMAL. One moment, before we go. We are now rich. Both my father and mother are fond of you—I love you, O my Little Dove of Duty and Devotion—I love you. Will you not marry me?
MORGIANA. I cannot tell. Not if it means a quarrel between you and your parents. Besides, we are not yet

44   A L I B A B A   [ACT II

safe. How can we speak of love when danger threatens us?

No. 12. DUET   ..   ..   KEMAL *and* MORGIANA.

During the last refrain, AL RASCHOUN *and* ROBBERS *creep in at the corners,* R. *and* L. *unseen, listening.* KEMAL *and* MORGIANA *withdraw singing, to the door, embrace, and enter the house together.* AL RASCHOUN *and* ROBBERS *move stealthily in, grouped* R.C. *and* L.C., *facing the house. They all raise their arms in a gesture of triumphant revenge, as :—*

the TABS *close.*

(NOTE : *As there is no scene change, a short Interval may be covered by music, or a dance, or refrain in front of* TABS.)

Scene 3.

Scene.—*The same.*

When the Curtain *rises again, it is just before the dawn. A party of revellers, men and women, come down the street, singing. This Number may be a Chorus only, or* Mustapha Nutha *and* Mustapha Dubbuhl *may have verses.*

No. 13.   Ensemble   ..   ..   ..   Revellers.

(*During the last refrain, the* Robbers, *who are concealed behind the stalls and in corners, steal out and mingle with the crowd. Business of picking pockets, etc. After the Number, the* Revellers *exeunt, singing, and the* Robbers *conceal themselves once more. Enter* Heelam, *rather drunk. He staggers to his stall, and lies down.* Al Raschoun *comes out of hiding and approaches him.*)

Raschoun. Friend cobbler, who has played this trick on me? (*He points to the crosses.*)

(Heelam *looks at the crosses and laughs.*)

Yes, that's a good joke, my friend, isn't it? Was it you?

Heelam. Me? Good heavens, no! I don't go about chalking on houses, though anything for a change, of course.

Raschoun (*suavely*). I'm sure you were clever enough to know the house again. Come, wasn't there a little chink in the bandage over your eye?

Heelam. Oh, yes, but the little widow was so sweet I hardly liked to mention it.

Raschoun. And—which house was it?

Heelam. A—ah!

Raschoun (*throwing him some money*). Which house?

Heelam (*pocketing the money*). That one! (*He points to* Ali Baba's *house.*)

(Al Raschoun *goes up to the house and throws open the door, goes inside and returns.*)

RASCHOUN. Empty! All gone! (*Coming down.*) Friend cobbler, at the other end of the town is the Tavern of Palms which opens at dawn. Go there, drink, and await me.

HEELAM. But I'm not thirsty!

RASCHOUN (*handling his dagger*). Go there!

HEELAM. Oh, well, anything for a change!

(*He hurries off* L.)

RASCHOUN. Hist!

(*The* ROBBERS *emerge.*)

Watch! Listen! Keep hidden! (*He makes a sign.*)

(*The* ROBBERS *hide again.* AL RASCHOUN *withdraws into the house. Enter* ALI BABA, SELIMA, KEMAL, MORGIANA *and* NELLA *up* L. *They are talking volubly, and group at* C.)

NELLA. But I ask you, Ali, I ask you, Kemal, Selima, what am I to do now? Cassim dead! I don't know what I'm going to do! I shall be so poor!

KEMAL. You can ask the Caliph for the widow's pension, can't you?

ALI BABA. Of course! Of course! Of course!

NELLA. No, Cassim never paid in for it. But if you, Ali, would give me a share of your wealth, I'd be provided for. After all, you went twice to the cave. Poor Cassim only went once, and then all he got was a dose of poison.

ALI BABA. What!

KEMAL. All you think of is money.

SELIMA. I agree. I think the time has come to tell Nella the truth.

ALI BABA. I agree. Nella, we had to be secret for a while. Cassim is not dead!

NELLA. Not dead? Oh, dear! But we've just buried him!

ALI BABA. No, that was a dummy. We have hidden Cassim in the new house I have bought. As soon as we feel the robbers have lost the scent and have given up the search, he will return to you.

NELLA. And I'll tell him something! He'll wish he had died!

(AL RASCHOUN *comes down* L. *of the group.*)

RASCHOUN (*bowing low*). Forgive me for interrupting, but I can see you are leaders of Society in Baghdad.
ALI BABA. Well, I wouldn't say *that*!
NELLA. *I* would! My husband is . . .
ALI BABA. Nella, please!

(*The others sign to her to be quiet.*)

In what way can we serve you?
RASCHOUN. I am Suda-Kaban, a rich merchant from Radaman—a cousin of the Sultan of Jam. Can you tell me where I may find shelter suitable to my station in life, and for my servants? I do not fancy a Tavern in Baghdad.
ALI BABA. Certainly! Certainly!
KEMAL. We have a fine new house!

(MORGIANA *puts her hand on his arm.*)

What is it, Morgiana?
MORGIANA. Nothing, my lord. (*She frowns at him. He is puzzled.*)
RASCHOUN. I am deeply grateful. If you could shelter us for the rest of the night. My horses and men are tired, and I would crave your hospitality for them also.
SELIMA. Well, the place isn't straight yet.
MORGIANA. It cannot be made ready until tomorrow.
ALI BABA. Morgiana, if I say it must be ready within an hour, then it must be ready.
SELIMA. But Ali . . .
ALI BABA. Away! Let us away! Am I not Ali Baba, the richest man in all Baghdad? Do I not have fine friends? A cousin of the Sultan? And a great house? And plates of gold? And fruits? And wine? And silks? And the best wife in Persia? Away!

No. 14. ENSEMBLE. "Ali Baba's Rich Today" (ALI *and* CROWD.)

(*Air :* " *Boys and Girls Come Out to Play.*")

CROWD. Salaam to Ali on his way
For Ali Baba's rich today
You never know, and it does no harm
To bob your noddle and say " Salaam " !
(*Chanting.*) Ah—ah! Ah—ah! Ah—ah AH!

(*Prostrating themselves.*)

ALI BABA. (*to* SELIMA).
You see, my dear, how the money talks
So spread the carpets—draw the corks!
(*To the* CROWD.)
Welcome, friends, for I bid you spend
At Baba Towers a long week-end!

CROWD (*chanting*). Ah—ah! Ah—ah! Ah—ah! AH!

(RASCHOUN *takes* SELIMA'S *hand,* ALI *takes* NELLA'S, *and they proceed off* R. *in procession, the* CROWD *following singing a repeat of the chanting.* KEMAL *is last. He turns to* MORGIANA, *who has paused.*)

KEMAL. Come, Morgiana!

(*He follows the others off, and* MORGIANA *moves to follow, then checks, in a pool of cold light.*)

MORGIANA. O Kemal Haroun, son of Ali! This is an evil hour!

She moves off, as, off-stage, the chorus is repeated fortissimo, and

The CURTAIN *falls.*

ACT III.

SCENE I.

SCENE.—*A room in* ALI BABA'S *house.*

When the CURTAIN *rises* ALI BABA *and* SELIMA *are seated up* C. SELIMA *is holding a long rope of pearls, letting them fall between her fingers lovingly. They come down* C.

SELIMA. Indeed, they are beautiful, O My Lord of Wealth and Wisdom.

ALI BABA (*taking the pearls from her and putting them round her neck*). Then it is a case of beauty to adorn beauty, O Date-Palm of Duty and Devotion!

SELIMA (*pleased with the compliment*). My lord is too good to me!

ALI BABA (*very tenderly, holding her by the shoulders and looking into her eyes*). Nothing is too good for goodness itself, O Citron of Seductive Sweetness! (*He draws her to him gently and kisses her.*)

No. 15. DUET . .. ALI BABA *and* SELIMA.

(*Enter* KEMAL *and* NELLA R.)

KEMAL. Father, I have established the stranger in the best guest chamber and have appointed two slaves to attend him. I ventured to offer these to him on your behalf.

ALI BABA. You did quite right, my boy, quite right.

NELLA (*excitedly to* SELIMA). He must be very wealthy. Out there in the courtyard is a retinue of servants big enough for the Caliph himself!

SELIMA. Oh, dear! I hope our poor hospitality will satisfy him.

KEMAL. Of course it will, mother. Didn't father buy another dozen slaves only yesterday? Great vats of wine? Mountains of fruit? And gallons of scented oil now warming for our baths?

ALI BABA. Besides, our Morgiana is equal to any situation. I think you may trust her to see to our distinguished guest, my dear.

NELLA. Remember I saw him first. If there are any tips left under the plates, they're mine!

SELIMA. Tips? Oh, be quiet, Nella! You're so *common!*

NELLA. Common! *Well!* Listen . . .

ALI BABA (*ignoring her*). Go and ask him in, Kemal, my son. It is discourteous to keep him waiting.

KEMAL. He has descended to the courtyard to give instructions to his men, father. I'll go and call him in now.

(KEMAL *goes off* C. SELIMA *anxiously pats her hair and shakes up some cushions.* ALI BABA *stands down* L. *in a dignified attitude.*)

NELLA. I was about to say . . .

SELIMA. Well, *don't!*

ALI BABA (*to* SELIMA). O Flower of Forbearance! (*To* NELLA.) O Mistress of Magnanimity! Hush! Our guest!

(*Enter* KEMAL, *followed by* AL RASCHOUN. *The latter pauses for a moment at the entrance, taking in the whole room and its occupants with one sweeping, penetrating glance.*)

KEMAL (*approaching* ALI BABA). Father, Lord Suda-Kaban of Radaman, our guest!

(*The two men bow to each other in a stiffly courteous way, then* AL RASCHOUN *goes to* SELIMA *and takes her extended hand and raises it to his lips. He is about to move away when* NELLA *gives a little jump forward with her hand extended also.* AL RASCHOUN *takes it and quickly slips one of the rings off and pockets it.*)

RASCHOUN (*softly as he bends over* NELLA'S *hand*). An old Persian custom! (*To* ALI BABA.) I hardly know how to thank you, my Lord Ali Baba. But for your offer of hospitality, I and my men would have slept on the cold, hard ground tonight with nothing but the stars above us.

ALI BABA (*gravely*). We are honoured that you deign to share our humble abode.

RASCHOUN. That is well said, sir. I shall not forget your taking ways.

NELLA. Oh, we are all like that in our family. If my poor Cassim were here, he'd do better than this. We had a grand house, running h. and c. in all the rooms, bed, bath and sitt. all in one and a special pipe line laid to the brewery!

ALI BABA. T'ch! T'ch! (*He draws* NELLA *away, protesting*.)

SELIMA. Morgiana shall see that you are well served, sir.

RASCHOUN. I am afraid I am putting you to a lot of trouble, O Lady of Loveliness and Liberality. You see, I am an oil merchant, and only this morning I bought forty large jars of oil. My men are unloading them from the horses now . . .

ALI BABA (*cutting him short*). No trouble at all, I assure you. Selima, my love, order Morgiana and her slaves to come here.

(SELIMA *goes to* R. *and claps her hands.* MORGIANA *comes in* R.C. *followed by* SLAVES *running* R. *and* L.)

MORGIANA. You called, mistress?

(*She looks full at* KEMAL *for a moment, then lowers her eyes*.)

SELIMA. Yes, we have an honoured guest, Morgiana. I want you to see that he has the best we have for his comfort.

KEMAL. And see that his servants are well cared for, Morgiana, and the horses stabled.

MORGIANA (*without raising her eyes*). Yes, my lord.

NELLA. And see that the scented oils are heated well— to bring out the smell.

SELIMA. The *aroma*!

MORGIANA. The oils already bubble above the fire.

ALI BABA. Let them cool gently.

(MORGIANA *turns to go*.)

Wait! We'll welcome our guest in proper style. Bring in some drinks, Morgiana.

(MORGIANA *and her* SLAVES *go* R. *and get small trays of glasses and drinks. They hand them round.*)

ALI BABA. Health to lord Suda-Kaban of Radaman! May his oil wells never run dry!

(*They all raise their glasses.*)

RASCHOUN (*acknowledging the toast*). To Ali Baba! And may the *source* of his wealth never give out!

NELLA. Oh, well, here's mud in your eye!

(SELIMA *nudges* NELLA *angrily. Business.*)

ALI BABA. Come, now, let's have singing, in welcome to our guest.

No. 16. CONCERTED NUMBER .. ALI BABÀ, SELIMA, NELLA *and* KEMAL.

AL RASCHOUN *joins in and Chorus of* SLAVES *led by* MORGIANA.

SELIMA. Let us have a special feast prepared for the guest, Morgiana.

NELLA. And don't forget my special diet. You know, sparrows' knees in aspic, washed down with a little of my special Three Star stomach medicine.

KEMAL. Morgiana will rise to the occasion, never fear.

MORGIANA (*looking at* AL RASCHOUN *strangely*). Yes—I shall rise to the occasion.

ALI BABA (*to* AL RASCHOUN). And now Morgiana will show you to your room, sir. Then you shall superintend the stabling of your horses yourself, and then—the feast! Remember, my slaves are yours to command.

(SLAVES *all salaam.*)

RASCHOUN (*meaningly, preparing to follow* MORGIANA *off* C.). I shall remember, Ali Baba. Suda-Kaban does not easily forget.

(*He exits with* MORGIANA, *followed by* SLAVES. ALI BABA *and* SELIMA *exeunt* R.)

NELLA. Oh, well, I'd better get into something striking for the occasion. (*Musing as she goes off* L.) Now, I wonder which will impress him most—the purple striped satin with the peacocks' feathers on it, or the emerald green silk shot with puce and yellow?

KEMAL (*sarcastically, as he stands alone down* R.C.). I should think either would knock him flat! (*He moves about restlessly.*) Oh, Morgiana, Morgiana! How I long for you!

(MORGIANA *enters* C. *and stands looking at him for a moment in silence, an expression of yearning on her face.* KEMAL *turns and sees her and she quickly puts a finger to her lips to warn him to be quiet. With a quick look* R. *and* L. *she comes down* C. *to* KEMAL.)

MORGIANA (*speaking urgently*). Kemal, I want you to promise me something.

KEMAL. You know I would promise you anything in the world, dear one. What is it?

MORGIANA. I want you to promise me that I shall be asked to dance at this feast tonight.

KEMAL (*puzzled*). Why, yes, that is an easy thing to promise. You dance so beautifully. But why this special request, my love?

MORGIANA. Don't ask me now—I can't tell you. (*She looks round fearfully.*) Someone might be listening, and I am afraid for you.

KEMAL (*suddenly reaching out and drawing her to him, laughing happily*). Silly little Morgiana! Always imagining things! You mustn't be afraid of anything while you have my love to protect you.

No. 17.   SONG   ..   ..   KEMAL.

(MORGIANA *slips from his grasp and dances around him tantalisingly as he sings.*)

The TABS *close.*

*During the Scene change :—*KEMAL *may sing the 2nd or 3rd Verse of his song, and this may be followed by a march cross-over of the* ROBBERS, *singing a reprise of the " Robbers' Song."*

The TABS *open.*

Scene 2.

SCENE.—*Interior of a stable.*

There is a row of large, tall jars along the back wall. One or two stools or a small bench.

When the CURTAIN *rises* AL RASCHOUN *is there with his* THIEVES. *He is pacing up and down angrily.*

RASCHOUN (*standing at* R. *and facing his men*). Now listen, men! You know Ali Baba is the man who discovered our secret, don't you?

ROBBERS (*in languid chorus*). Aye, master. (*They all yawn.*)

RASCHOUN (*moving up* C.) That was his brother, Cassim, I killed in the cave. (*Turning, and speaking to the group* L.) Now Ali Baba must suffer the same fate.

ROBBERS. Aye, kill him! Kill him! (*Yawns.*)

SMASHEM (R.). Couldn't we just give him a good telling-off instead?

GRABBEM (R.). How about putting a notice on the cave door, " Trespassers will be prosecuted "? That ought to stop 'em!

RASCHOUN (*thunderously*). Silence, you half-wits, or you'll share Ali Baba's doom!

(SMASHEM *and* GRABBEM *crouch behind the others.*)
Now, you have got your last instructions. You are to hide in those jars until I give you the signal to come out, then you are to rush into the banquet chamber, kill Ali Baba—and his son and his wife, too, if they try to interfere. (*He rubs his chin thoughtfully.*) Morgiana, I think we will capture. She is a pretty little thing and will be useful.

ROBBERS (*with sinister laughs and nudges*). Mmmm . . . mmm . . . Yes!

RASCHOUN (*sharply*).
   Now! To your posts, and not another sound!
   For woe betide you if you should be found!

(*He strides off* L.)

ROBBERS. Yippee!

(*They yawn and all get into the jars, through the concealed doors behind them, during which there is soft Music—The Robbers' Chorus motif. This changes to "Morgiana" music as* MORGIANA *enters* R. *She has two large vases for oil. She claps her hands twice. Two* SLAVES *enter* L.)

MORGIANA. Fill this jar with oil for lamps.
SLAVE (*taking it*). Yes, lady.
MORGIANA. Fill this one with warm scented oil for the bath of our guest.
2ND SLAVE. Yes, lady. (*He takes the other vase.*)
MORGIANA. Is the oil for cooking heated, Olaka and Omomo?
SLAVES (*together*). Yes, lady.
MORGIANA. Attend me presently, with those vases filled. I would rest.
SLAVES. Yes, lady.

(*They run out* L.)

No. 18. SONG .. .. MORGIANA.
(*This song should be of a lullaby type.*)

(*As the Number ends, snores are heard from within the jars.*)

MORGIANA. Oh dear, those horses are noisy creatures—they must be terribly tired.

(*Tremendous snores.*)

Oh! That wasn't horses! It came from the jars! (*She mounts a stool or bench and peers into a jar.*) Oh! A man! Sleeping! (*She goes to others.*) Another man! (*She repeats the business.*) Another! (*Coming down.*) The slaves of the so-called oil merchant! Forty! The Forty Thieves—asleep! Very well, Al Raschoun! Your disguise will not save you! Slaves! (*She claps her hands.*)

(*The* SLAVES *enter* L.)

MORGIANA. Have you filled the jars?
SLAVES. Yes, lady!

MORGIANA. Empty them! Fill them again, and others, with hot—boiling—cooking oil! See that it bubbles—steams—smokes! Quickly!

(*The* SLAVES *run off* L. *There are increasing snores from within the jars.*)

    Snore on, Rapacious Robbers of Raschoun!
    Ended your days of toil!
    You cannot rob, or kill, from night to noon—
    Or even snore—when boiled in oil!

(*The* SLAVES *return with three steaming pitchers.*)

    Come! Copy me! Fill every jar full up!
    And then again—on oil shall they sup!

(MORGIANA *and the* SLAVES *fill the jars. Terrible shrieks and groans issue from them.*)

    Come, hurry! Never dawdle! Never potter!
    And let the next instalment be—much hotter!

(*She is filling jars—shrieks rise—and the* SLAVES *hurry out with empty vases, as* SMASHEM *and* GRABBEM *emerge unhurt from their jars,* R.C. *Unseen by* MORGIANA, *they throw up their hands and rush off* R.)

Make haste!

The SLAVES *return with filled vases. They rush to the jars and continue filling them as—*

    The TABS *close.*

MORGIANA *may sing a Reprise of No.* 18, *or, if comedy is required, an additional* DUET *may be introduced for* DUBBUHL *and* NUTHA.

Scene 3.

Scene.—*In* Ali Baba's *house, as for Scene 1, Act III.*

When the Curtain *rises, Music. The feast is prepared.* Al Raschoun *is on the stage alone, looking very pleased and humming jauntily to himself as he examines various " objets d'art " and pockets one or two.*

Enter Smashem *and* Grabbem *r.c. They come in with exaggerated stealth, looking from left to right and saying " Ps-s-s-t ! " continually.*

Raschoun. What's the matter with you two pocket imitations of honest robbers ? Do you imagine you're disguised as cats ? Get back to your barrels !

Smashem (*looking all round, behind curtains, pictures, etc.*). His-s-s-t ! You are in dire danger !

Grabbem (*looking under cushions and going on hands and knees and squinting along the floor*). Death may be lurking anywhere ! Ow ! (*He gets up quickly as* Al Raschoun *aims a kick at his rear.*)

Raschoun. Stop acting like a couple of comic opera policemen and tell me what you're getting at !

Smashem ⎫ (*together*). Well, you see, we were . . . .
Grabbem ⎭ (*They stop and bow to each other politely.*)
Smashem. After you, Grab !
Grabbem. After you, Smash !

(Al Raschoun *loses patience and strides towards them and grabs them each by the collar.*)

Raschoun (*holding one in each hand*). Now, I'll give you half a minute to make up your minds who tells me before I bang your heads together, and I warn you, the splinters'll fly !

(Smashem *and* Grabbem *quake and mouth at each other.*)

Smashem (*hoarsely*). After you, dear boy, I'm through.

Grabbem (*starts to say "After you— " then catches sight of* Al Raschoun's *face and gives a little high-pitched croak*). Well, it's like this 'ere, I mean " here "—self and partner regret to have to inform you t-that—

SMASHEM (*getting it out in a rush*)—all the others are dead!
RASCHOUN. WHAT? (*He releases them so suddenly that they fall backwards.*)
GRABBEM. Dead—moribund—liquidated.
SMASHEM. Stone-cold! Smoking like mad when we left 'em!
GRABBEM. Boiled well and truly in oil by as pretty a little oil boilerer as ever you clapped eyes on!
RASCHOUN (*almost hissing through his teeth*). Morgiana! That . . .
SMASHEM }
GRABBEM } (*together*). Ah-ah-ah!
RASCHOUN. Very well, it remains for me to carry out my revenge alone! (*Raising both hands and shaking his fists.*) And I swear it shall be done! Ali Baba *shall* die!

(*As he utters the last dire threats* SMASHEM *and* GRABBEM *look at him, scared, and silently creep off* R.C. *while he is not looking. Enter* ALI BABA, SELIMA *and* KEMAL C.)

ALI BABA (*genially*). Ah, all alone, my lord? Our guests are just arriving, so we shall soon have some music—entertainment—feasting . . . (*He indicates the divan.*)

(AL RASCHOUN *sits. Enter* GUESTS. *They group themselves about the stage. Enter* NELLA, *very gorgeous and bejewelled*, HEELAM *and* MUSTAPHA NUTHA *and* MUSTAPHA DUBBUHL, *the two latter very resplendent and overdressed. Comic business of entrance.*)

No. 19. CHORUS .. .. .. FULL COMPANY.

(*At the end of this Number, the* GUESTS *seat themselves on cushions on the floor.* SLAVES *enter, led by* MORGIANA, *and begin to wait on them with trays of fruit, wine, etc. It is soon evident that two of the " slaves " are* SMASHEM *and* GRABBEM *in disguise, the clothes being too big for them.*)

KEMAL. Can we not have Morgiana to dance for us while we are feasting, father?

(AL RASCHOUN *looks up sharply.*)

ALI BABA. By all means! (*He claps his hands.*) Morgiana!

(MORGIANA *runs to him and prostrates herself before his divan.*)

Dance for us, Morgiana. Dance for us some wild delirious dance of daring Dervish derivation!
MORGIANA (*rising*). The Dagger Dance!
ALL (*in a tremendous shout*). The Dagger Dance!

(MORGIANA *comes to* C. *Slaves group about her. Cymbals clash. She poses* C. *drawing a dagger. The* SLAVES *dance as if they, too, held daggers.*)

No. 20. THE DAGGER DANCE .. MORGIANA *and* SLAVES

(*The dance starts quietly, but rises in a mysterious and sinister manner to a wild climax. At the climax,* MORGIANA, *with a shriek, leaps at* AL RASCHOUN *and stabs him to the heart. He falls dead. There is a great shout. All rise, and then stare in horror, silent.*)

ALI BABA (*after the pause*). Morgiana! What have you done? You must be mad to kill our honoured guest!
MORGIANA (*throwing the dagger down, lifting her head and looking straight at* ALI BABA). I have killed, not Suda-Kaban of Radaman—but Al Raschoun, the Robber Chief of the Forty Thieves!
ALL. Al Raschoun!
MORGIANA. Within an hour he meant to kill *you*, my lord, instead! Look! (*She swiftly goes to* AL RASCHOUN *and takes from his robes a long, wicked-looking dagger.*) He tricked you! He is the owner of the cave! He is the one who poisoned Lord Cassim!
KEMAL (*going to her*). Morgiana! So brave and wonderful!
ALI BABA (*clapping his hands and pointing to* AL RASCHOUN). Away with that—*carrion*! Indeed have I been foully deceived!

(SLAVES *run to* AL RASCHOUN *and carry him out* R. *One* SLAVE *remains. He goes up to* NELLA.)

CASSIM. Nella!
NELLA. Cassim! My little Cassim! (*They embrace.*) I didn't know you!
CASSIM. I hardly know myself in these! Me! In Second-hands!
NELLA (*aside*). Wait till I get you home! Going and drinking poison instead of attending to business ...
ALI BABA. Enough! All have been saved! How can we reward our Morgiana here?
KEMAL (*stepping forward*). By letting me marry her, O my father.
SELIMA. Kemal!
KEMAL. Yes, my mother! Release her from slavery and let her be my wife.
MORGIANA. For we have loved each other such a long time.
ALI BABA. Yes, let them wed!

(*There are cries of delight from the* GUESTS. KEMAL *and* MORGIANA *embrace.*)

NELLA. After all, she'll only be exchanging one kind of slavery for another. (*To* CASSIM.) Sit *down*, Cassim, and don't *wriggle*!
SELIMA. I wish them every joy—I'm so happy! (*Weeping.*) I do love a real good cry!
ALI BABA. No! Laughter! Singing! Wine! Music! A marriage dance!

(*Cheers and laughter and chattering.*)

M. DUBBULH. And while we're at it—I offer half a crown, a bit of string, and a packet of chewing gum for this young lady (*bringing forth* GOGETTI) whom I propose to marry forthwith!
NELLA. You shan't!
M. NUTHA (*bringing forward* ROSETTI). One and tenpence, a trouser button and my photo for this lot! Wedding tomorrow!
NELLA. You can't!

(*The two couples embrace.*)

ALI BABA. They *shall*! Three weddings in one day! For threes bring luck to all!

(SMASHEM *and* GRABBEM *enter up* C., *curiously disguised.*)

SMASHEM
GRABBEM } *(together).* What about us?

(*The whole company "boo" them loudly.*)

Thank you! Most encouraging! (*They march down to* R. *and* L. *corners of the stage.*)

The FULL COMPANY *move down and group.*

No. 21. GRAND FINALE .. Medley of Choruses ..
FULL COMPANY.

CURTAIN.

FURNITURE AND PROPERTY PLOT.

ACT I.

SCENE 1.

Six "stalls" (*set as in ground plan*) with Oriental awnings.

(*These to be provided with property goods appropriate to the various trades.*)

Personal :

HEELAM : Sandals for repair. Cobbler's tools.
CASSIM : Money. (*In an Oriental purse.*)
MORGIANA : Packages of food, water bottles, etc.

Sundry :

Rugs, silks, fruit, water bottles, etc., for itinerant traders in the Chorus.

SCENE 2.

Two "boulders" set below ground row, for seats.

Personal :

ALI : Food packages, water bottle. (*From previous scene.*)
KEMAL : Ditto.
SMASHEM : Necklace.
GRABBEM : Packet of tea.

Sundry :

Jewels, bundles, silks, boxes of treasure, etc., for the Robbers.
Curved sword for AL RASCHOUN and daggers for the Robbers.
Sack of gold, various jewels, silks, etc. IN CAVE, for ALI on entrance from the cave.

SCENE 3.

Set as for Scene 1. Awnings over stalls lowered.

Personal :

SNAKE CHARMER : Trick snake in box.
ALI and KEMAL : Treasure, from previous scene.

ACT II.

SCENE 1.
Boulders as before.
Robbers' weapons as before. A jar, or skin bottle of wine, and two cups for one of the Robbers.
AL RASCHOUN: A small phial of powder.
Set within the cave: A small litter, to carry CASSIM.

SCENE 2.
Set as for Act I, Scene 1.
Personal:
MORGIANA: Black scarf as bandage.
AL RASCHOUN: Money.
On HEELAM'S stall: Two or three pieces of white chalk.

SCENE 3.
Set as for Act I, Scene 3. (Awnings lowered.)
Personal:
AL RASCHOUN: Money.

ACT III.

SCENE 1.
One rostrum. (*Up* C.) Rugs on the floor.
Three Eastern divans. (*Set as in ground plan.*)
Cushions on divans. Oriental draperies and hangings.
Wine cups, jars, fruit bowl, dishes of sweetmeats, set about the divans.
Personal:
SELIMA: Rope of pearls.
SLAVES: Trays of wine, sweetmeats, etc.
AL RASCHOUN: Long dagger, concealed in robes.

SCENE 2.
Several tall oil jars. (*See Production notes.*)
Personal: MORGIANA: Two jars for boiling oil.

SCENE 3. As for Scene 1.
Personal: MORGIANA: Dagger for "Dagger Dance."

LIGHTING PLOT.
ACT I.

SCENE 1.

All circuits full in floats and battens.
F.O.H. flood 36 lavender and 51 gold.
Straw floods behind exists. NO CUES.

SCENE 2.

Floats and battens, pink and gold FULL.
Sky-cloth flooded No. 18 blue, full.
F.O.H. to flood C. area No. 51 gold.
CUE: ALI.—" Never more. Never more will I enter ... "
Fade all floats and battens slowly, and focus F.O.H. gold to a spot on the cave, for pause before exit and curtain fall.

SCENE 3.

Floats pink and blue only, at ½.
Battens ditto at ¾. No. 4 amber floods on exits.
F.O.H. flood straw. Add 51 goldspot on ALI BABA for Song. (No. 8.)
CUE: *As* SNAKE CHARMER *begins to chant*: Fade all pink. Fade F.O.H. flood. Spot CHARMER moonlight blue. (*Return to opening lighting after Dance and Crowd exeunt.*)

ACT II.

SCENE 1.

To open: Black out. (SPIRITS *on ridge of ground row ready*.)
AT MUSIC CUE: Fade in No. 18 blue flood on cloth for silhouette. Follow with F.O.H. moonlight blue faded in on stage for Ballet. Spot as desired.
End of Ballet: Fade all to B.O. for exeunt. (*Flood to fade last, for silhouette picture.*)
Follow with: F.O.H. blue spot on CASSIM (*who has entered during B.O.*)
CUE: SPIRITS *exeunt as horses are heard*: Bring in floats and battens blue, slowly. Follow with F.O.H. flood 36 lavender, frost, and 51 gold frost, on C. area.

CUE : *As* ALI *and* MORGIANA *emerge from cave with litter :* Fade all slowly except blue in battens for exit, and tabs close.
In front of tabs : Moonlight blue spots on SPIRITS.

SCENE 2.
Lighting as for Act I, Scene 1.

SCENE 3.
To open : Floats :   Blue only at ½.
Battens : Blue only at ¾.
F.O.H. spot REVELLERS 36 lavender for Chorus.
After Number : Follow with pink in floats and battens, slowly, and then gold ditto as scene proceeds. F.O.H. flood 36 lavender.
CUE : *As* KEMAL *exits after the Crowd and Principals :* Fade all fairly quickly. Focus F.O.H. 36 lavender flood to a spot on MORGIANA for curtain.

ACT III.

SCENE 1.
All circuits in floats and battens, full.
F.O.H. flood 36 lavender and 51 gold.
No. 4 amber floods behind entrances.
Spot No. 36 lavender for Numbers as desired.

SCENE 2.
Floats and No. 1. Batten : Gold and blue, only.
F.O.H. flood straw.
CUE : *During " boiling oil " business :* Fade all except blues in floats and batten. Change F.O.H. flood for blue, focused on C. area.

SCENE 3.
Lighting as for Scene 1.
Spot MORGIANA 36 lavender and No. 7 rose for " Dagger Dance," during which floats and battens to be well checked down.
CUE : *As* COMPANY *shout* " Al Raschoun " (*following* MORGIANA'S *line*) bring up lighting as before, full.

www.ingramcontent.com/pod-product-compliance
Lightning Source LLC
LaVergne TN
LVHW051707080426
835511LV00017B/2785